Scripture Mastery Sonnets

By Tom Matkin
©2014
Cardston, Alberta

Explanation

The LDS Seminary program focuses on 100 scriptures that students are asked to memorize, understand and use to learn and teach the gospel. Recently those scripture choices were revised and when it came to my attention I decided to have a close look at the new list. There are 25 related to each of the 4 years of study in the Seminary curriculum. Basically, with a few exceptions, the breakdown is naturally scriptures from the Old Testament, New Testament, Book of Mormon and Doctrine and Covenants. One of my ways of pondering and studying scriptures is to reflect upon a passage or verse by writing a sonnet about it.   As I worked my way through these scriptures, one at a time, I was able to produce about 150 sonnets. In the course of this I published the sonnets into 4 separate thin volumes and now I'm publishing the whole works into one book.

I recommend this process as a means of internalizing and teasing out the meaning of scripture. But if you don't have the time or inclination to write your own sonnets, I hope you enjoy mine.

Tom Matkin
March, 2014

Dedication

To Betty for tolerating my obsessions and supporting every good thing.

Contents

Old Testament Scripture Sonnets
Pages 1-44

New Testament Scripture Sonnets
Pages 45-77

Book of Mormon Scripture Sonnets
Pages 78-106

Doctrine & Covenants Scripture Sonnets
Pages 107-171

Old Testament

Moses 1:39 For behold, this is my work and my glory - to bring to pass the immortality and eternal life of man.

Sonnet 679 Moses 1:39

Our God who set the universe in space
Who organized the stars and planets too
Who put the sun and moon and earth in place
Did all of this and more for me and you.

Our God who crafted gardens, rocks and hills
Who made the ice, the raindrops and the dew
Who gathered seas and oceans, lakes and rills
Did all of this and more for me and you.

Our God who sent his Son to die to win
And overcome the fall and to renew
His spirit children from both death and sin
Did all of this and more for me and you.

And gave us prophets, prayer and parents too
And all of this and more for me and you.

Moses 1:39
For behold, this is my work and my glory—to bring to pass the immortality and eternal life of man.

Sonnet 499 Moses 1:39 (#2)

That battle that began before this time
Is all about the agency of man
It's not a point that's subtle or sublime
You choose your fate by picking out a plan.

The one is mis'ry all dressed up as fun
The rebel call in irony complete
By disobedience their fates undone
They lose it all by opting for a cheat.

The other is surrender to a way
That works a mighty paradox of love
Your freedom found by learning to obey
A Father who defends you from above.

His work and glory tied to your success
His focus is entirely to bless.

Moses 7:18 And the Lord called his people Zion, because they were of one heart and one mind, and dwelt in righteousness; and there was no poor among them.

Sonnet 680 Moses 7:18

Well, how to be united heart and soul
When pride and selfish interests inspire?
We must, as many, make one common goal
Conforming to the truth and not desire.

Well, how to overcome the bane of sin
When evil's so ubiquitous and strong?
We must in humble attitude begin
By cleansing our own vessel of all wrong.

Well, how to do away with poverty
When programs seem in vain and overpriced?
We must be sure that all our charity
Is rooted in the purest love of Christ.

One thing for sure in search of Zioness
Success depends on personal progress.

Sonnet 500 Moses 7:18 (#2)

It's hard to even dream of such a place
Where everyone is of one heart and mind
And where there is not even any trace
Of anything unrighteous or unkind.

And more that even that I find it hard
To fathom life without the poor around
No weak, no foolish, and no lame or scarred
No low, no slow, no simple and no clown.

No hungry and no hostages of fate
No puny or pathetic hanging back
No beggars and no blind to contemplate
No lazy with their lives all out of whack.

And where to you suppose that you will be
When Zion is declared to be poor-free?

Abraham 3:22-23
22 Now the Lord had shown unto me, Abraham, the intelligences that were organized before the world was; and among all these there were many of the noble and great ones;
23 And God saw these souls that they were good, and he stood in the midst of them, and he said: These I will make my rulers; for he stood among those that were spirits, and he saw that they were good; and he said unto me: Abraham, thou art one of them; thou wast chosen before thou wast born.

Sonnet 681 Abraham 3:22-23

Don't get too focused on the here and now
Don't take the pain and joys of each day
And set them as a feature you endow
With undeserved eminent display.

Don't get me wrong the present knows us best
In fact, the moment's all we really own
And nothing can be changed or done to wrest
Control from its uncompromising throne.

But still to not attend to what was done
Or fail to point or plan or pray ahead
Would be to not anticipate the sun
Because a night has put your day to bed.

So navigate the present with intent
To reach the future heaven's past has sent.

Genesis 1:26-27
26 ¶And God said, Let us make man in our image, after our likeness: and let them have dominion over the fish of the sea, and over the fowl of the air, and over the cattle, and over all the earth, and over every creeping thing that creepeth upon the earth.
27 So God created man in his own image, in the image of God created he him; male and female created he them.

Sonnet 682 Genesis 1:26-27

All things denote there is a God above
The beauty and the order which abound
The majesty of mountains and of love
The music and variety of sound.

And added to the miracle of birth
And firmaments that glorify His hand
And all the other evidence of earth
Is God's averment all of this was planned.

So stand in awe of touch and sounds and sights
That quicken in our nature worship's ken
But also in your heart receive the rites
That comfort, teach and testify to men.

Thus you must pray to find, as I have done
Your witness of the Father. And the Son.

Sonnet 683 Genesis 1:26-27 (#2)

It should not be a stretch of any sort
To understand the way this all played out
What other image could a child sport?
A son should mirror his Father without doubt.

So now the common looking glass displays
The face of God for anyone to see
And so in wonderment we ought to gaze
And find there our potentiality.

If all you see is just you looking back
Or worse, a hardened mask of selfishness
Repent and get yourself back on the track
To claim your heritage of godliness.

"His image in your countenance" expounds
Inheritance that knows no earthly bounds.

Sonnet 684 Genesis 1:26-27 (#3)

There are some scary animals at large
The jungle cats, the rhinos and the like
And whales as big as almost any barge
And sharks and snakes with venom in their strike.

But nothing else is dominant like man
Who has a way with weapons unsurpassed
And who by dint of following a plan
Subdues all other species first to last.

So nothing really challenges man's place
Nor could it since God planned it out that way
It suits His purpose for the human race
To have this gift so agency's in play.

So being unafraid of any other
Has left man free to terrify his brother.

Genesis 2:24
24 Therefore shall a man leave his father and his mother, and shall cleave unto his wife: and they shall be one flesh.

Sonnet 685 Genesis 2:24

Before the Ten Commandments were in stone
Well, just as soon and Eve and Adam were
They were enjoined to go through life alone
Thus marriage is the life we should prefer.

And we can tinker with this if we will
And choose perhaps to never even leave
But if we do we'll never quite fulfill
The blessings of obedience to cleave.

And something that I'll teach you from my heart
There's nothing in this life as good as this
Not money, fame or power as a start
Compares in any way to wedded bliss.

And add to this a child or two or more
And life has given all you could ask for.

Genesis 39:9
9 There is none greater in this house than I; neither hath he kept back any thing from me but thee, because thou art his wife: how then can I do this great wickedness, and sin against God?

Sonnet 686 Genesis 39:9

Temptation can be countered and denied
And passions can be bridled and controlled
But sometimes you must run from troubles side
In haste, in strength, to break the tempters hold.

And in the grasp is not the moment to
Consider all the wrongness of that course
As best we can we ought to work it through
Before the hand of evil grabs full force.

Decide today your avenues of flight
And better still determine to avoid
The places where enticements likely might
Be cultivated, sanctioned and enjoyed.

Temptation can be properly withstood
When we plan out the how of being good.

Exodus 19:5-6
5 Now therefore, if ye will obey my voice indeed, and keep my covenant, then ye shall be a peculiar treasure unto me above all people: for all the earth is mine:
6 And ye shall be unto me a kingdom of priests, and an holy nation. These are the words which thou shalt speak unto the children of Israel.

Sonnet 687 Exodus 19:5-6

Hell's Angels and the Asian gangs and such
Rotarians and Kinsmen and the like
And former Army buddies stay in touch
While bowling leagues maintain the right to strike.

It's all about belonging to a group
For safety, friendship, fun and profit too
We tend to want to be within the loop
Of those we feel some kind of kinship through.

And never mind those rabid sports team fans
Or politics or music devotees
Or unions, buffs or fishermen or clans
We all belong to one or more of these.

But one stands out in treasure and in trust
Belonging to the fold of God's a must.

Sonnet 688 Exodus 19:5-6 (#2)

On Sunday in the pews and wide awake
Reviewing and renewing by degree
Commandments and the covenants we make
The Church is where the saints of God should be.

In harmony and hope throughout the week
Our hearts and hands united in the plea
To care and bless and be among the meek
The Church is where the saints of God should be.

In meetings or in visits or in class
In songs of praise or quiet bended knee
To see beyond this world's darkened glass
The Church is where the saints of God should be.

A treasure seeker's solemn guarantee -
The Church is where the saints of God should be.

Exodus 20:3-17

3 Thou shalt have no other gods before me.

4 Thou shalt not make unto thee any graven image, or any likeness of any thing that is in heaven above, or that is in the earth beneath, or that is in the water under the earth:

5 Thou shalt not bow down thyself to them, nor serve them: for I the Lord thy God am a jealous God, visiting the iniquity of the fathers upon the children unto the third and fourth generation of them that hate me;

6 And shewing mercy unto thousands of them that love me, and keep my commandments.

7 Thou shalt not take the name of the Lord thy God in vain; for the Lord will not hold him guiltless that taketh his name in vain.

8 Remember the sabbath day, to keep it holy.

9 Six days shalt thou labour, and do all thy work:

10 But the seventh day is the sabbath of the Lord thy God: in it thou shalt not do any work, thou, nor thy son, nor thy daughter, thy manservant, nor thy maidservant, nor thy cattle, nor thy stranger that is within thy gates:

11 For in six days the Lord made heaven and earth, the sea, and all that in them is, and rested the seventh day: wherefore the Lord blessed the sabbath day, and hallowed it.

12 ¶Honour thy father and thy mother: that thy days may be long upon the land which the Lord thy God giveth thee.

13 Thou shalt not kill.

14 Thou shalt not commit adultery.

15 Thou shalt not steal.

16 Thou shalt not bear false witness against thy neighbour.
17 Thou shalt not covet thy neighbour's house, thou shalt not covet thy neighbour's wife, nor his manservant, nor his maidservant, nor his ox, nor his ass, nor any thing that is thy neighbour's.

Sonnet 689 Exodus 20:3-17

When people as a group or one on one
Decide to live without a moral law
The seeds of awful misery thus begun
Will lead those people to a tragic flaw.

And founding fathers wisely have not failed
To see the wisdom of the Maker's tools
And codes and constitutions are detailed
To follow more less these ten best rules.

Still time goes on and nations seem to stray
As principles are compromised and tossed
Until the love of sinning wins the day
And laws are changed and peace and safety lost.

So even as our legal systems fail
Make sure, for you, that these commands prevail.

Sonnet 691 Exodus 20:3-17 (#2) Thou shalt have no other gods before me.

On scales of one to ten where ten is best
And one is really really really dumb
This number one commandment beats the rest
A ten, and first among all rules of thumb.

And yet we get temptations not a few
To put the dumbest things ahead of God
And stumble in the first of what to do
By choosing secondary paths to trod.

Examine what you do from hour to hour
Or day or week or month or year or more
And see if you incorporate the power
Of having put no other God before.

So carefully prioritize your way
And do it every time you kneel to pray.

Sonnet 692 Exodus 20:3-7 (#3) Thou shalt not make unto thee any graven image

It's fine to put a picture on your wall
As long as it's not something you adore
It's fine to make a drawing or a scrawl
As long as it's not something you implore.

And you can even make a graven thing
And put it in your living room for fun
But don't be thinking it will ever bring
Good luck, or happiness, or battles won.

And don't be bowing down at any cost
Before the things that hands have ever made
Or serving anything that's been embossed
Cause God gets angry when He's been betrayed.

Look to the law and to the prophets too
And God will show his mercy unto to you.

Sonnet 692 Exodus 20:3-37 (#4) Thou shalt not take the name of the Lord thy God in vain

Though swearing and expletives are just wrong
Yet many seem in love with the profane
And loose their filthy tongues in word and song
Thus showing coarse and vacuous disdain.

And vanity exhibited this way
May even hide behind more gentle talk
So this commandment covers what we say
And also has to do with how we walk.

For how can anyone be truly right
In keeping God ahead in their domain
Or serve and worship Him both day and night
If wilfully they take his name in vain?

So keeping score along commandment trail -
If you don't keep the third the others fail.

Sonnet 693 Exodus 20:3-17 (#5) Remember the sabbath day, to keep it holy.

And I thank heaven for the Sabbath day
A challenge for me one day of the week
To use the time in such proper way
To make it holy, restful and unique.

So many now will work or play at will
Or shop or do their housework just as rote
And seldom even think to try to fill
The day with anything of worthy note.

And so this gift of glory goes unclaimed
And lost to legions who by NFL
Or beach or such distractions surely framed
Their narrow reach to things terrestrial.

Please make you sign of faith by Sabbath days
That celebrate and bless in holy ways.

Sonnet 694 Exodus 20:3-17 (#6) Honour thy father and thy mother

Our parents come in every shape and size
Invisible, invasive or inane
Inadequate, inactive or unwise
And humble, true, indifferent and vain.

And some are rich, solicitous and kind
And others greedy, poor and hard to please
And many best described as unrefined
While others climb the social scale with ease.

And yet no matter where your parents fit
In goodness or in evil or in place
You honour them by living bit by bit
Above the fortunes of your family base.

Until if everyone would turn this key
The world would be a better place to be.

Sonnet 695 Exodus 20:3-17 (#7) Thou shalt not kill.

My Hebrew is as weak as weak can be
But I can study out a word or two
And sometimes, in my weakness, I can see
That English words in scripture aren't quite true.

The origin of "kill" is such a case
In English it's as broad as broad can be
And much more than the murder of the race
It could include the swatting of a flea.

But this translation isn't really right
The Hebrew word is narrowly defined
To cover only homicidal spite
The wanton sorts of murder of mankind.

For good advice on killing as a sport
I recommend you study this report.*

*Fundamental Principles to Ponder and Live
President Spencer W. Kimball, Ensign, Nov. 1978, 43
https://www.lds.org/general-conference/1978/10/fundamental-principles-to-ponder-and-live?lang=eng

Sonnet 696 Exodus 20:3-17 (#8) Thou shalt not commit adultery

Of all the common villainies of man
Of all the things self evidently low
Of all the things against which we should plan
Adultery is as bad as man can go.

Of all the common virtues of a man
Of all the things self evidently great
Of all the things for which we ought to plan
Fidelity's the loftiest estate.

Companion virtues that attend the blessed
Are loyalty and chastity and love
With modesty and decency they best
Encompass what true goodness consists of.

Determine now to find and keep the way
That guards against temptations to betray.

Sonnet 697 Exodus 20:3-17 (#9) Thou shalt not commit adultery

Beyond the common meaning of the word
In Hebrew and by inference in play
Is a commandment needing to be heard
To not pollute your worship any way.

Apostasy is quite the ancient threat
As old and new as sexual designs
Devotion to the Lord must be well set
Adulterated worship undermines.

Thus chasing after gods of stone or gold
Is much the same as faithlessness to wife
As this commandment covers, we are told
The unadulterated view of life.

So if you want full blessings in your house
You must be true to God and to your spouse.

Sonnet 698 Exodus 20:3-17 (#10) Thou shalt not steal.

I read this law as wide and very strong
Entailing every breach of honesty
Forbidding almost any kind of wrong
And not just grand or petty larceny.

And focus on the things that theft involves
And not just on the money or the stuff
And soon a host of thieveries evolves
Until each honest robber shouts "Enough!"

There's reputation high up on the list
And time and trust and peace of heart and mind
And hope and promise too should not be missed
When things purloined are honestly defined.

And we should pray in faith each time we kneel
To be forgiven for the things we steal.

Sonnet 699 Exodus 20:3-17 (#11) Thou shalt not bear false witness

This happens all the time in courts of law
And sadly in the parliaments of man
And even will some research people draw
False witness to defend their science plan.

This means that much of what we have for laws
And all the trials heard from day to day
Are tainted by these testimony flaws
And truth and consequence are gone astray.

But most of us don't have a day in court
Or testify to congress anyway
Or make or publish findings of import
We just go on with living day to day.

But still we have the chance to break this law
When gossiping becomes our lowly flaw.

Joshua 24:15
15 And if it seem evil unto you to serve the Lord, choose you this day whom ye will serve; whether the gods which your fathers served that were on the other side of the flood, or the gods of the Amorites, in whose land ye dwell: but as for me and my house, we will serve the Lord.

Sonnet 700 Joshua 24:15

Sometimes the truth is elegantly found
And stated in a way that clears the mind
And this, a declaration so profound
Is of that elegant and truthful kind.

The fundamental answer to this test
Should be as Joshua has said so well
"I'll serve the Lord ahead of all the rest.
And any other master I'll repel."

And if you take you family on this course
And covenant in sacred binding ways
You'll wed your feeble efforts to a Force
That makes a glory of your earthly days.

You fought the war in heaven for this right
So make and keep this choice with delight.

1 Samuel 16:7
7 But the Lord said unto Samuel, Look not on his countenance, or on the height of his stature; because I have refused him: for the Lord seeth not as man seeth; for man looketh on the outward appearance, but the Lord looketh on the heart.

Sonnet 701 1 Samuel 16:7

There seems to be a market for good looks
There's lotions and there's potions and there's gels
There's surgery enough to fill up books
And it seems like almost any option sells.

Add in tattoos and liposuction too
And jewelry and wigs and botox shots
And there is almost nothing we won't do
To change appearances that life allots.

Does anyone remember in this haste
To mutilate with plastic body art
That God is unimpressed with such a waste
His vision being focused on the heart.

Don't fret or worship at your looking glass
It didn't come to stay, it came to pass.

Psalm 24:3-4
3 Who shall ascend into the hill of the Lord? or who shall stand in his holy place?
4 He that hath clean hands, and a pure heart; who hath not lifted up his soul unto vanity, nor sworn deceitfully.

Sonnet 702 Psalm 24:3-4

I wouldn't like to judge another's heart
Or even make a judgement of his hands
But much of common culture and its art
Must even seem unclean to total fans.

So much of what is popular is vain
And wickedness and narcissism rules
And more and more, embracing the profane
Is standardized procedure for these fools.

But you should want to stand above this waste
To climb towards the Lord for His embrace
Be clean and pure and temperate and chaste
Empowered by His everlasting grace.

So make your stand for holiness succeed
Through cleanliness in every word and deed.

Psalm 119:105
105 Thy word is a lamp unto my feet, and a light unto my path.

Sonnet 703 Psalm 119:105

We know from writ that God is Word and Light
The light and life of every man from birth
That darkness comprehended not the sight
Of light that shineth over all the earth.

And this is light and knowledge so profound
That metaphor explodes into the real
All meaning and direction can be found
Because of what the word and light reveal.

So move your feet and scurry on your way
Employing as you go in faith the lamp
That shows the only path in night or day
Upon which faithful saints should want to tramp.

He is the Way, the Word, the Light, the Lamb
The Truth, the Rock, the Bread, the Life, the Lamp.

Psalm 127:3
3 Lo, children are an heritage of the Lord: and the fruit of the womb is his reward.

Sonnet 704 Psalm 127:3

Most miracles are very soon forgot
If even ever noticed as they came
But even interventions humbly sought
May burn a while then die out like a flame.

And some rewards are quickly gone away
There's some we eat and others that get broke
And some get lost or simply go astray
Or tossed in trash or go straight up in smoke.

But children are an everlasting gift
A miracle eternal owned and named
And even if they stray or go adrift
Their spirits can through sealings be reclaimed.

When all is said and done for time on earth
The family is the thing of greatest worth.

Proverbs 3:5-6
6 In all thy ways acknowledge him, and he shall direct thy paths.
7 Be not wise in thine own eyes: fear the Lord, and depart from evil.

Sonnet 491 Proverbs 3: 5-6
(With apologies to George Macdonald and C.S. Lewis)

The natural man, and I mean "he", not "she"
Is loath to seek directions on his way
Although he may find map reading a key
His instinct is to try each path in play.

And preference for going his own way
To even being on the better track
Can set into his nature day by day
Until he's lost all want for coming back.

And since he now has not the will to say
In truth and love to God, "Thy will be done"
Then God will sadly say to him some day
In truth and love,"Thy will be done, my son."

Oh grant me strength to ask, to plead to know
The path for me that God would gladly show.

Isaiah 1:18
18 Come now, and let us reason together, saith the Lord: though your sins be as scarlet, they shall be as white as snow; though they be red like crimson, they shall be as wool.

Sonnet 705 Isaiah 1:18

The beauty and the poetry of this
The red and white and crimson and the wool
Togetherness as kind as any kiss
The scarlet and the reasoning with snow.

A message of eternal love and hope
An invitation reconciling sin
Atonement in its meaning and its scope
A melody to cancel all chagrin.

Come now, come now, come now. The plea
The parent pleading, promising and mild
Come now, don't wait, come now and be-
Come pure and clean, and mine, beloved child.

The sweetest kindest invitation yet
An everlasting life without regret.

Isaiah 5:20
21 Woe unto them that are wise in their own eyes, and prudent in their own sight!

Sonnet 706 Isaiah 5:20

Like toddlers out in traffic we cavort
In constant mortal danger unobserved
Our safety measures always falling short
Unless we take direction gladly served.

There's two great dangers blind us on the road
The first, that devil monster blowing smoke
Befuddlement his navigation mode
He wants to blind, to bind, and even choke.

But even worse, perhaps, is self defeat
The wilful blindness of the proud and vain
The child who thinks he's smart about the street
And holds all wise correction in disdain.

But God provides a wise and prudent way
For everyone who chooses to obey.

Isaiah 29:13-14

13 Wherefore the Lord said, Forasmuch as this people draw near me with their mouth, and with their lips do honour me, but have removed their heart far from me, and their fear toward me is taught by the precept of men:

14 Therefore, behold, I will proceed to do a marvellous work among this people, even a marvellous work and a wonder: for the wisdom of their wise men shall perish, and the understanding of their prudent men shall be hid.

Sonnet 707 Isaiah 29:13-14

I would not dwell upon the reasons why
Or vanity of lips and mouths of men
Or darkness even of the noonday sky
To those whose hearts have lost what should have been.

Instead I marvel at what is restored
What wisdom, work and wonderment is come
This great and awesome undeserved reward
Of infinite from out a finite sum.

I revel in the revelations won
I marvel in the miracles attained
I tremble in the temples of the Son
I preach of prophets prayerfully sustained.

All this will end the wisdom of the wise
As Israel gathers to receive its Prize.

Isaiah 53:3-5

3 He is despised and rejected of men; a man of sorrows, and acquainted with grief: and we hid as it were our faces from him; he was despised, and we esteemed him not.

4 Surely he hath borne our griefs, and carried our sorrows: yet we did esteem him stricken, smitten of God, and afflicted.

5 But he was wounded for our transgressions, he was bruised for our iniquities: the chastisement of our peace was upon him; and with his stripes we are healed.

Sonnet 513 Isaiah 53:3-5

Some words are deep and heavy, wise and strong
With meanings that add feelings to insight
That lift from common prose to lovely song
And generate a special truth and light.

"Grief" and "sorrow", are such weighty terms
And "sticken", "smitten" and "afflicted" too
And "bruised" and "wounded", in a word, confirms
The sacrifice that was atonement's due.

And for us words of equal weight and strength
As we are offered "peace" by what he did
And added to our peace we're "healed" at length
Through his "chastisement" in this awful bid.

It's a good deal for us, by any test
He bears our transgressions and we get blessed.

Isaiah 58:6-7
6 Is not this the fast that I have chosen? to loose the bands of wickedness, to undo the heavy burdens, and to let the oppressed go free, and that ye break every yoke?
7 Is it not to deal thy bread to the hungry, and that thou bring the poor that are cast out to thy house? when thou seest the naked, that thou cover him; and that thou hide not thyself from thine own flesh?

Sonnet 708 Isaiah 58:6-7

The root of all discipleship is this
To bridle all your passions with restraint
To discipline yourself and to dismiss
The urges that disqualify a saint.

And so to navigate from deadly sins
Like gluttony and greed and lust and wrath
And envy, sloth and pride a saint begins
By fasting as a tool to find the path.

And as you use this offering to share
Some bread, some shelter and some clothing too
This simple key unlocks the vault of prayer
And pours out heaven's blessings upon you.

This fasting is a win win thing for sure
You build yourself and also bless the poor.

Isaiah 58:13-14

13 If thou turn away thy foot from the sabbath, from doing thy pleasure on my holy day; and call the sabbath a delight, the holy of the Lord, honourable; and shalt honour him, not doing thine own ways, nor finding thine own pleasure, nor speaking thine own words:

14 Then shalt thou delight thyself in the Lord; and I will cause thee to ride upon the high places of the earth, and feed thee with the heritage of Jacob thy father: for the mouth of the Lord hath spoken it.

Sonnet 709 Isaiah 58:13-14

What are the odds of winning Powerball
Or taking Bingo or Blackjack by storm?
What is the chance of being born real tall
Or being strong much more than just the norm?

Are you the lucky one who wins at cards
Or hits a homerun ball with simple ease?
Do you write sonnets better than the Bard's
Or can your charm bring scoffers to their knees?

It's things like this that happen to a few
Not everyone is blessed with luck like that
And almost never will it work for you
But there's a sure thing no one could lose at.

Just keep the sabbath holy through and through
And God will bless you more than luck could do.

Jeremiah 1:4-5
4 Then the word of the Lord came unto me, saying,
5 Before I formed thee in the belly I knew thee; and before thou camest forth out of the womb I sanctified thee, and I ordained thee a prophet unto the nations.

Sonnet 710 Jeremiah 1:4-5

When God calls anyone to do his best
At almost anything we do in church
That one is set apart and fully blessed
As he embarks upon his holy search.

And ancient prophets were, or so we're told
Ordained before they even came to earth
Thus called and their positions well foretold
In blessings given long before their birth.

And don't you think when your time came as well
When you were you but not yet born of man
But ready for a time on earth to dwell
That you were also ordained to a plan?

And that your greatest challenge is to find
And follow what your God thereby assigned.

Ezekiel 37:15-17

15 The word of the Lord came again unto me, saying,

16 Moreover, thou son of man, take thee one stick, and write upon it, For Judah, and for the children of Israel his companions: then take another stick, and write upon it, For Joseph, the stick of Ephraim, and for all the house of Israel his companions:

17 And join them one to another into one stick; and they shall become one in thine hand.

Sonnet 711 Ezekiel 37:15-17

A "quad" is pretty heavy, really thick
But you can lift and hold it with one hand
A modern version of Ezekiel's stick
Exactly as the Lord had said He planned.

This scripture is prophetic evidence
Of forethought and compassion and of love
A testimony of benevolence
That blesses down below from up above.

The Bible and Book of Mormon thus
In harmony and love and power too
Unite to offer this eternal plus
That God planned all of this for me and you.

But none of this will help or bless a lick
Unless you take the time to read the stick.

Amos 3:7
7 Surely the Lord God will do nothing, but he revealeth his secret unto his servants the prophets.
Amos 3:7

Sonnet 515 Reflections on Amos 3:7

Who doesn't love to learn of secret things
Like truthful treasures, valuable and rare
That's why they market those decoder rings
To those who want both secrets and to share.

And peeping wizards too and magic men
WIll make a claim to special powers of sight
By checking out your tea leaves now and then
Or gazing into certain stars by night.

Yet even if these sorceries were true
No value to the information found
Has ever been confirmed upon review
Such secrets being patently unsound.

But God reveals his secrets one by one
To prophets before anything is done.

Malachi 3:8-10

8 Will a man rob God? Yet ye have robbed me. But ye say, Wherein have we robbed thee? In tithes and offerings.

9 Ye are cursed with a curse: for ye have robbed me, even this whole nation.

10 Bring ye all the tithes into the storehouse, that there may be meat in mine house, and prove me now herewith, saith the Lord of hosts, if I will not open you the windows of heaven, and pour you out a blessing, that there shall not be room enough to receive it.

Sonnet 712 Malachi 3:8-10

In law the punishment is extra strong
And earns another measure of disgust
If someone's theft or hurt or harm or wrong
Is classified in crimes as "breach of trust".

That's when we have the care and keeping of
Something for someone else in our affairs
And we betray their confidence and love
By taking for ourselves what's really theirs.

And most of us would understand this end
And never want to be among the cursed
Who cheat or hurt their very trusting friend
Those sorts we number as the very worst.

Yet everything we have is as a trust
And God asks only that we share a crust.

Sonnet 713 Malachi 3:8-10 (#2)

It can't be wise to steal from God above
And punishment for such an awful thing
Though ministered in fairness and in love
Would have to be a fire and brimstone thing.

So I would sooner focus on the good
The promise to the payer of his tithes
Make sure I've well and fully understood
What God has said will be the payers prize.

So here's a little list of things I've heard
Insurance against all the fires of hell
And blessings both abundant and preferred
Protection, peace and confidence as well.

And if God's window's open, well that's when
There is a better chance you might see in.

Malachi 4:5-6
5 Behold, I will send you Elijah the prophet before the coming of the great and dreadful day of the Lord:
6 And he shall turn the heart of the fathers to the children, and the heart of the children to their fathers, lest I come and smite the earth with a curse.

Sonnet 714 Malachi 4:5-6

I did some temple work just yesterday
For people born four thousand years ago
And in my heart a moment of dismay
For why this work can be so very slow.

And later on I watched a fresh recruit
Her eyes filled up with kind and happy tears
Kneel silently and gather in the fruit
Of hearts now joined from independent spheres.

And then I thought of couples who that day
As proxies for the dead renewed their vows
There eyes and hearts and hands a grand display
Of blessings only such a place allows.

The temple is that turning point for me
Where my heart turns to where it ought to be.

Sonnet 750 Malachi 4:5-6 #2

Could simple curiosity explain
This yearning to complete my family tree
To fill in all the links that make the chain
Of life that led, at last, to little me?

These mysteries and challenges pertain
To wrack me with this awful need to know
What is it that I hope to find or gain
Why is it that I work this puzzle so?

There's more than just the finding, I declare
There's something so exquisite with this pain
It's how my heart has softened through this care
A gift of love I almost can't contain.

For as I search and widen out my scope
Somehow my loss is overcome by hope.

Sonnet 752 Malachi 4:5-6 #3

Elijah came to Kirtland with the keys
And things began to change across the earth
Societies for genealogies
At last and first were wisely given birth.

Elijah came to Kirtland with the keys
And angels of assistance were unleashed
And spirits in a sort of long deep freeze
Could hope and know they now could be released.

Elijah came to Kirtland with the keys
And you still have the choice. "What to do?"
But if you choose to turn your heart to these
Your Fathers' will, in turn, be turned to you.

Elijah came to Kirtland with keys
And brought a curse of darkness to its knees.

New Testament

Matthew 5:14-16
14 Ye are the light of the world. A city that is set on an hill cannot be hid.
15 Neither do men light a candle, and put it under a bushel, but on a candlestick; and it giveth light unto all that are in the house.
16 Let your light so shine before men, that they may see your good works, and glorify your Father which is in heaven.

Sonnet 733 Matthew 5:14-16

The virtue of humility is great
A deep and solemn duty of the saint
This opposite of pride-fulness and hate
A friend to love and cousin to restraint.

Yet sometimes it's confused with lesser traits
The reticent, the shy, the timid souls
May think they're humble in their fearful states
Denying the great weakness of these roles.

There's hidden selfishness in holding back
In guarding for yourself against the night
In failing to be kind with those who lack
The joys and the blessings of your light.

So gather up your courage and step out
And let your gospel light shine all about.

Sonnet 734 Matthew 5:14-16 (#2)

How many of us bathed in gospel light
Ordained, baptized and blessed by sacred rite
Deny the breadth, the power and the height
By keeping such a blessing out of sight?

And do we realize our common plight
That having now been blessed with heaven's light
And should we then refuse to fight the fight
We thus commit an unforgiving slight?

And how hard can it be in such a night
With truth and beauty shining ever bright
To sing, to talk, to shout, to share, to write
And glorify the Father with our light?

Forever have the holders of this light
Been told to shine it forth with all their might.

Matthew 11:28-30
28 ¶Come unto me, all ye that labour and are heavy laden, and I will give you rest.
29 Take my yoke upon you, and learn of me; for I am meek and lowly in heart: and ye shall find rest unto your souls.
30 For my yoke is easy, and my burden is light.

Sonnet 505 Reflections on Matthew 11: 28-30

The yoke has been a genius way to pack
As long as any cargo has been hauled
You cannot share the power of legs and back
Unless some sort of harness is installed.

And best to be yoked up with someone strong
Enough to lighten any sort of weight
Someone whose help is never slight or wrong
Who offers peace and rest without debate.

And burdens much more grave than gravity
Like sin and loss and grief and death and pain
Are carried in that endless cavity
That such a yoke can lift without a strain.

Why heap your burdens in a careless pile
When He would help you carry them in style?

Matthew 16:15-19
15 He saith unto them, But whom say ye that I am?
16 And Simon Peter answered and said, Thou art the Christ, the Son of the living God.
17 And Jesus answered and said unto him, Blessed art thou, Simon Bar-jona: for flesh and blood hath not revealed it unto thee, but my Father which is in heaven.
18 And I say also unto thee, That thou art Peter, and upon this rock I will build my church; and the gates of hell shall not prevail against it.
19 And I will give unto thee the keys of the kingdom of heaven: and whatsoever thou shalt bind on earth shall be bound in heaven: and whatsoever thou shalt loose on earth shall be loosed in heaven.

Sonnet 735 Matthew 16: 15-19 But whom say ye that I am?

If you would want a temple recommend
Or to be baptized or to be ordained
Then you will be expected to attend
An interview before this is obtained.

And such will be the pattern of the hour
That you will hear this question with your call
"Do you believe through inspiration's power
In Jesus Christ the Savior of us all?"

And all will hinge upon an answer true
The build, the opening, the keys, the ties
That bind and loose. It flows from how you do
With this grand quest. The interviewer's prize.

The Bishop's question echoes in your ear
"Whom say ye that I am?" is what you hear.

Sonnet 736 Matthew 16:15-19 (#2) Thou art the Christ

And so the only answer is this one
This vivid, short, expression of a fact
This testimony of the Father's Son
In simple words, straight forward, and exact.

He is the Christ! The Savior of us all
And such a declaration stands alone
As truth upon which nations rise and fall
The ultimate, the crowning stepping stone.

And every man or woman ever born
Is blessed by this atoning agent's love
Invested with the chance to share His scorn
Then take a mansion with Him up above.

And everyone can know that this is true
That's everyone. That's me. That's them. That's you!

Sonnet 737 Matthew 16:15-19 (#3) Flesh and Blood
Hath Not Revealed It

The air is full of messages of hope
Of testimony singing in the wind
Beyond all flesh and blood in power and scope
A balm, a joy, a rescue for the sinned.

The witness is a universal thing
The signal ever strong and sharp and true
A light, a burning feeling and a sting
A dream, a gift, delightful as the dew.

But flesh and blood can easily resist
Distract, forget, deny and even lie
It's sinful pleasures cannot coexist
With revelation beyond earth and sky.

So be believing and enjoy the rain
Of wisdom flesh and blood cannot obtain.

Sonnet 738 Matthew 16:15-19 (#4) Upon this Rock I Will Build My Church

The church of God must ever have its seer
Be led in mercy by a prophet's hand
A revelator who can feel and hear
And pass in love to others God's command.

And vital as it is to have this head
A prophet seer and revelating rock
If followers can ever be misled
That still could be a fatal stumbling block.

So each and every member needs this gift
And gets it by the laying on of hands
To have the Holy Ghost to teach and lift
And guide him through the worst of life's demands.

And standing ever at the door, the Rock
Invites us all to open to His knock.

Sonnet 739 Matthew 16:15-19 (#5) The Keys of the Kingdom

The concept and the substance of a key
Is matched or messaged in this simple word
The opposite or foil, plain to see-
Where there's a key, a "lock" must be inferred.

While earthly doors and gates are often locked
And keys required to pass through such a wall
There's something much more seriously blocked
And that's the tree of life beyond the fall.

And sin and death and misery yield up
Their hold, to keys the Master forged in pain
Unlocking as He chose the bitter cup
Each banished child from Adam's ball and chain.

And now the Master locksmith shares these keys
With almost countless priesthood appointees.

Sonnet 740 Matthew 16:15-19 (#6) Bind on Earth –
Bound in Heaven

In heaven there are passages we know
That will not lock or yield to any key
Except such key be wielded here below
Upon the force of heavenly decree.

Why can't a child be baptized up above
Or temples be among the mansions there
Why must some things be tied or let go of
Down here before God blesses the affair?

I have to think the answer would be clear
If memories of heaven were not sealed
But since we have no recall of that sphere
We have to go with just what's been revealed.

And that gives so much meaning to life's day
Perhaps that's why He worked it out this way.

Matthew 22:36-39

36 Master, which is the great commandment in the law?

37 Jesus said unto him, Thou shalt love the Lord thy God with all thy heart, and with all thy soul, and with all thy mind.

38 This is the first and great commandment.

39 And the second is like unto it, Thou shalt love thy neighbour as thyself.

Sonnet 741 Matthew 22:36-39

If you would know and keep these two commands
There is no better recipe or school
No better explanation of demands
Than what we call the Savior's Golden Rule.

And also there are parables He taught
That put some extra flesh upon this bone
See what the Good Samaritan has brought
Or think of Sheep and Goats before the throne.

Or you could do a quick review of things
That give you so much joy you lose the cost
If such that turn your mind or pull heart strings
Are selfish or just vapid then you're lost.

The only true and lasting lifetime art
Is serving God and man with all your heart.

Matthew 28:19-20
19 ¶Go ye therefore, and teach all nations, baptizing them in the name of the Father, and of the Son, and of the Holy Ghost:
20 Teaching them to observe all things whatsoever I have commanded you: and, lo, I am with you alway, even unto the end of the world. Amen.

Sonnet 742 Matthew 28:19-20

There's Superman and Spiderman and Hulk
There's Power Rangers, X Men and much more
These comic superheros come in bulk
With umpteen super powers in the corps.

The notion of abilities beyond
All mixed up with a "good and evil" fight
And triggered by a cape or costume donned
Will fill most any fan with great delight.

And yet we know there's nothing of the kind
Like Yeti and the unicorn or such
These heroes are just constructs of the mind
Imagination overworked too much.

But put a mission badge on any one
And God will make him super til he's done.

Luke 24:36-39

36 ¶And as they thus spake, Jesus himself stood in the midst of them, and saith unto them, Peace be unto you.
37 But they were terrified and affrighted, and supposed that they had seen a spirit.
38 And he said unto them, Why are ye troubled? and why do thoughts arise in your hearts?
39 Behold my hands and my feet, that it is I myself: handle me, and see; for a spirit hath not flesh and bones, as ye see me have.

Sonnet 743 Luke 24:36-39

The promise of a resurrection day
Is in those marks upon His hands and feet
The evidence He overcame the clay
And rose in death's inglorious defeat.

And more so is the promise to us all
That resurrection counts for us as well
And if we heed to heaven's loving call
We'll rise above the chains of death and hell.

And if you sing that your Redeemer lives
And pray in secret for confirming grace
And ponder on the wisdom scripture gives
And all His kind and good commands embrace.

Then you will find within as proof sincere
A peace that passeth every mortal fear.

John 3:5
5 Jesus answered, Verily, verily, I say unto thee, Except a man be born of water and of the Spirit, he cannot enter into the kingdom of God.

Sonnet 744 John 3:5

There is a Father of your spirit soul
The Great and Grand eternal God of all
Whose work and glory is to make you whole
An heir to life eternal's homeward call.

And you were born of earthly parents too
And so a second father came to be
A gift to make your days both long and true
A branch to seal you to a family tree.

And water and the Spirit give effect
To third rebirth, that miracle of grace
The only way to cleanse and to perfect
The sinner who would seek the holy place.
And when reborn, by this third Father claimed
Commanded and remembered and renamed.

John 14:6
6 Jesus saith unto him, I am the way, the truth, and the life: no man cometh unto the Father, but by me.

Sonnet 745 John 14:6

We sometimes glide across important words
Not stopping to determine what they mean
But I say pay attention to all thirds
Because they signal places we should glean.

Sometime ago I figured, just for me
That "study" "pray" and "work" engendered most
Of all the concepts bundled up by three
And my response is thereby diagnosed.

So Christ as "way" and "truth" and "life" reminds
Me of those duties that I sometimes shirk
And of the faithful triplet thread that winds
Through all of prayer and study and of work.

Yes He's the way, the truth, the life and so
My study, prayer and work will need to grow.

John 14:15
15 ¶If ye love me, keep my commandments.

Sonnet 746 John 14:15

Commandments are a blessing from on high
The inside scoop on how to live your days
Precautions against trouble coming nigh
A compass to direct all means and ways.

Commandments are a blessing from the Lord
Decoding all the mysteries of life
Protection much more potent than the sword
A shield against a world of constant strife.

Commandments are a blessing for the wise
A coach, an aide, a help, a lift, a right
A gift, a boon, a good, a strength, a prize
A way, a truth, a life, a rock, a light.

Commandments are a blessing from above
The means for God and man to share their love.

John 17:3
3 And this is life eternal, that they might know thee the only true God, and Jesus Christ, whom thou hast sent.

Sonnet 509 John 17:3

It's all in who you know, they sometimes say
In pointing out this commonest of trends
For those who hand out favours have a way
Of serving first the needs of their best friends.

And even God insists that you know him
And Jesus Christ, begotten only son
And this is no negotiable whim
Without it your eternity's undone.

And such a deal might seem a bit unfair
To those who find no joy in knowing God
But since his invitation is to share
The justice of the choice is no façade.

The tender mercy of the Prince of love
Will freely lift each willing friend above.

Acts 2:36-38
36 Therefore let all the house of Israel know assuredly, that God hath made that same Jesus, whom ye have crucified, both Lord and Christ.
37 ¶Now when they heard this, they were pricked in their heart, and said unto Peter and to the rest of the apostles, Men and brethren, what shall we do?
38 Then Peter said unto them, Repent, and be baptized every one of you in the name of Jesus Christ for the remission of sins, and ye shall receive the gift of the Holy Ghost.

Sonnet 747 Acts 2:36-38

The sequence here is classic one, two, three
First, there's the who, the what, the where, the when:
God made the Christ and plain for all to see
This sacred Son was crucified by men.

And second there's the consequence of sin
The problem or the tension of the plot
"What shall we do?" we offer with chagrin
"We're in the wrong, and tortured by the thought."

Then thirdly there is resolution found
The answer to our anguish can be heard
Remission and the loosing of the bound
Through loving invitation from the Word.

Repent and be baptized my sin-bound friend
And all can be forgiven in the end.

Acts 3:19-21

19 ¶Repent ye therefore, and be converted, that your sins may be blotted out, when the times of refreshing shall come from the presence of the Lord;

20 And he shall send Jesus Christ, which before was preached unto you:

21 Whom the heaven must receive until the times of restitution of all things, which God hath spoken by the mouth of all his holy prophets since the world began.

Sonnet 748 Acts 3:19-20

How many converts in the crowd, we ask
And just a few will "show of hand" reply
While those baptized at eight or so will bask
In the delusion such does not apply.

And some, in fact, neglect the effort to
Become converted, turned, and penitent
And then as their unblotted sins accrue
They lose the way and will to then repent.

Conversion isn't culture or good taste
It isn't learning jargon or routines
It's being born anew, and laying waste
To natural man and all his natural means.

Born in the Church, I hasten to maintain
Is not the same as being "born again".

Sonnet 749 Acts 3:19-20 #2

It's cool to be a part of something fresh
To be upon the cutting edge of change
To be an actual witness in the flesh
To something that's momentous or that's strange.

And better still to make a faithful note
Of how you felt and what you saw and heard
That someday people reading what you wrote
Will have a better sense of what occurred.

And so take notice of this rolling stone
That fills the earth with restoration's views
In every writ and prophet's message shown
As earth and heaven's greatest ever news.

You are a witness to this grand event
The preparation for the Lord's descent.

1 Corinthians 6:19-20
19 What? know ye not that your body is the temple of the Holy Ghost which is in you, which ye have of God, and ye are not your own?
20 For ye are bought with a price: therefore glorify God in your body, and in your spirit, which are God's.

Sonnet 751 1 Corinthians 6:19-20

So you, who could not fix a broken straw
Or unify all physics, large and small
Or make a spider's web or keep the law
Or beat the common cold or city hall.

So you, a helpless babe to start your days
Impatient, unconcerned and uninformed
Are blessed beyond your merit in the ways
The functions of your body are performed.

This body made with such exquisite skill
This miracle of purpose and of art
This engine of your wants and needs and will
This agent of the mind and of the heart.

You didn't build or even have intent
The Maker made this temple, you just rent.

Sonnet 753 1 Corinthians 6:19-20 #2

And then there is that "body beautiful"
The worshipping of tans or abs or hair
The tender care of every cuticle
And so much of ado with "what to wear".

And some will body-build or run for hours
Or cleanse and fast or gorge and purge and such
They focus all their time and all their powers
On sculpting or renewing over much.

Some other out of balance some will choose
Neglect, abuse, or sloven carelessness
Or mutilating piercings or tattoos
A bad attempt at metamorphosis.

Your body is a temple, fair or plain
But temple worship's something else again.

1 Corinthians 15:20-22
20 But now is Christ risen from the dead, and become the firstfruits of them that slept.
21 For since by man came death, by man came also the resurrection of the dead.
22 For as in Adam all die, even so in Christ shall all be made alive.

Sonnet 754 1 Corinthians 15:20-22

The logic of the resurrection plan
Is flawless as it weaves between the roles
Of God and Christ and Adam and of man
But logic doesn't capture hearts and souls.

It's Handel wrote the music to this song
And legions sing and listen to its airs
It's time, my friend, for you to sing along
To testify to what the writ declares.

For "Since by Man Came Death" is what it's called
"MESSIAH" Forty Six in Handel's book
A piece by which you will be so enthralled
I bet, I urge, I promise, "Have a look!"

And learn to feel, to shout, to sing, to cry
"In Christ shall all be made alive!" that die.

1 Corinthians 15:40-42

40 There are also celestial bodies, and bodies terrestrial: but the glory of the celestial is one, and the glory of the terrestrial is another.

41 There is one glory of the sun, and another glory of the moon, and another glory of the stars: for one star differeth from another star in glory.

42 So also is the resurrection of the dead. It is sown in corruption; it is raised in incorruption:

Sonnet 755 1 Corinthians 15:40-42

It's snowing as I read this verse today
The sun, the moon, the stars…, seem out of reach
And glory seems so very far away
I'm asking, "What does stormy weather teach?"

These clouds will test my faith, it seems to me
And fog will clog the memory of light
And even wind distracts so I don't see
The heavens as they are, though still in sight.

The thing is that I must, on cloudy days
Remind myself of what I really know
The sun, the moon, the stars…, those glory ways
Are waiting there for me beyond the snow.

And when I keep my faith through stormy days
My resurrected glory's bound to raise.

Galatians 5:22-23
22 But the fruit of the Spirit is love, joy, peace, long-suffering, gentleness, goodness, faith,
23 Meekness, temperance: against such there is no law.

Sonnet 756 Galations 5:22-23

The harvest of the Spirit in your days
Is love and joy and peace and patience too
And gentleness and goodness in your ways
To make a faithful, meek and temperate you.

While yielding to the flesh throughout your life
Will drive away the Spirit and replace
All love and joy with wickedness and strife
Long suffering and meekness with disgrace.

There is a constant battle for your soul
Between the Spirit and the lusts of man
And fruits of goodness ought to be your goal
So here's a wise and certain harvest plan.

Whatever kind of fruit you want to grow
Is governed by the seeds you choose to sow.

Ephesians 4:11-14
11 And he gave some, apostles; and some, prophets; and some, evangelists; and some, pastors and teachers;
12 For the perfecting of the saints, for the work of the ministry, for the edifying of the body of Christ:
13 Till we all come in the unity of the faith, and of the knowledge of the Son of God, unto a perfect man, unto the measure of the stature of the fulness of Christ:
14 That we henceforth be no more children, tossed to and fro, and carried about with every wind of doctrine, by the sleight of men, and cunning craftiness, whereby they lie in wait to deceive;

Sonnet 757 Ephesians 4:11-14

The officers are there to steer you right
To brace you from those winds that push and pull
They keep you from the cunning and the sleight
Protecting you from wolves in clothes of wool.

Your bishop and your president of stake
The prophet and the other brethren there
Will mark the safest path without mistake
Give them your faith and confidence and prayer.

The member who will love his leaders well
Is grateful for the the things that they advise
And will not criticize God's personnel
Is safest from deceit and crafty lies.

Perfecting of the saints is the design
And that can't happen when they're out of line.

Philippians 4:13
13 I can do all things through Christ which strengtheneth me.

Sonnet 758 Philippians 4:13

For better or for worse, in thick or thin
In good times or in bad, or sink or swim
Like Sister Wirthlin, Paul says with a grin
That "Come what may and love it" works for him.

And this is not a boast of Paul's own strength
But rather an expression of delight
That he could take life's blows to any length
Through Christ who saves at any depth or height.

And all the weak and weary can abound
And all the high and mighty be abased
Through Christ they all can happily be found
United in a strength by heaven graced.

Whatever is your circumstance or test
When you endure through Christ you'll come out best.

2 Thessalonians 2:1-3
1 Now we beseech you, brethren, by the coming of our Lord Jesus Christ, and by our gathering together unto him,
2 That ye be not soon shaken in mind, or be troubled, neither by spirit, nor by word, nor by letter as from us, as that the day of Christ is at hand.
3 Let no man deceive you by any means: for that day shall not come, except there come a falling away first, and that man of sin be revealed, the son of perdition;

Sonnet 759 2 Thessalonians 2:1-3

The prophet Paul saw better far ahead
Than most of men today see looking back
He understood the weaving of the thread
That signals heaven's angle of attack.

There is a detailed plan of all these days
The seasons and the centuries defined
The dispensations, ages and delays
All organized, predicted and aligned.

And so of course the time we call our own
This final restoration of all things
These latter-days were wisely, kindly shown
In prophesies declared on angel's wings.

And so we see foretold, revealed and planned
The day of Christ's return is close at hand.

2 Timothy 3:15-17

15 And that from a child thou hast known the holy scriptures, which are able to make thee wise unto salvation through faith which is in Christ Jesus.

16 All scripture is given by inspiration of God, and is profitable for doctrine, for reproof, for correction, for instruction in righteousness:

17 That the man of God may be perfect, throughly furnished unto all good works.

Sonnet 769 2 Timothy 3:15-17

If Twitterland and Instant Messageville
Is where you live each minute of the day
With brevity, the all consuming skill
Is that enough to help you on your way?

Or maybe you have earbuds locked in place
With lists of songs you simply have to play
So melody and rhythm fill your space
Is that enough to help you on your way?

But if you make a quiet time for God
A time to read from scripture every day
To be corrected, taught and even awed
Is that enough to help you on your way?

The wisdom of your Maker, I would say
Can't be discovered any better way.

Hebrews 12:9
9 Furthermore we have had fathers of our flesh which corrected us, and we gave them reverence: shall we not much rather be in subjection unto the Father of spirits, and live?

Sonnet 770 Hebrews 12:9

If reverence is hard for you to take
And being subject makes you ill at ease
Or if correction of a clear mistake
Is worse to you than any dread disease.

If you're with those who say they'd rather die
Than be subjected to parental will
Well that's a rule to which you will comply
As such a death-wish does the law fulfill.

Obedience means life or death to man
You choose to live when choosing to obey
And sadly in the vast eternal plan
The disobedient don't go that way.

It's up to you, but this advice I give
Be subject to the Father's will... and live.

James 1:5-6
5 If any of you lack wisdom, let him ask of God, that giveth to all men liberally, and upbraideth not; and it shall be given him.
6 But let him ask in faith, nothing wavering. For he that wavereth is like a wave of the sea driven with the wind and tossed.

Sonnet 771 James 1:5-6

The answers are no problem. They come fine
For giving wisdom liberally's the task
That marks the mission of the great Divine
But what we have to do, in faith, is ask.

And every honest convert knows the drill
To offer earnest prayer as Joseph did
And finds when "nothing wavering" the thrill
That warm embracing answer to his bid.

And children raised where Joseph's story's taught
May be believing all throughout their youth
But such a faithful childhood comes to nought
Unless they make their own request for truth.

If you still lack the wisdom that you need
Go ask in faith. An answer's guaranteed.

James 2:17-18
17 Even so faith, if it hath not works, is dead, being alone.
18 Yea, a man may say, Thou hast faith, and I have works: shew me thy faith without thy works, and I will shew thee my faith by my works.

Sonnet 772 James 2:17-18

The argument continues even now
On one side, "born again" and "saved by grace"
And on the other "work" and "hand to plough"
And each will find some writ to make their case.

It's true, of course, that Christ has done it all
That no one earns salvation on his own
And nothing else releases from the fall
That each must bow, in faith, before His throne.

And yet the sheep and goats are sorted plain
By what they do for others and their Lord
And sermons and His parables explain
That one must give of all he can afford.

Without both faith and works, your faith is dead.
That should have put the argument to bed.

1 Peter 4:6
6 For for this cause was the gospel preached also to them that are dead, that they might be judged according to men in the flesh, but live according to God in the spirit.

Sonnet 773 1 Peter 4:6

Each year the teaching pool among the dead
Is raised by 50 million more or so
The volume of the task, it must be said
Ensures the work will be there when you go.

And even down on earth the count goes up
As birthing beats the dying day by day
And so that work too overflows its cup
You're needed in a missionary way.

So preaching to the living and the dead
Amounts to quite a job, I have to say
And clearly we won't ever get ahead
Until that bright millennial array.

And since there's so much of this work to do
How wonderful it's joyful, through and through.

Revelation 20:12
12 And I saw the dead, small and great, stand before God; and the books were opened: and another book was opened, which is the book of life: and the dead were judged out of those things which were written in the books, according to their works.

Sonnet 774 Revelation 20:12

What's with this opened book of life I see
The one for works both well or poorly done
How can it miss the most and best of me
My list of good intentions one by one.

So many good things that I meant to do
Should count for something on the judgment day
My heart was pure, my thinking oh so true
My wants and wishes ever on display.

And I was always generous to a fault
In noticing the pressing needs of men
I should not be denied my place exalt
Because I could not make some time for them.

I do not think a judgment is ideal
That seems to favour those whose works are real.

Book of Mormon

1 Nephi 3:7
7 And it came to pass that I, Nephi, said unto my father: I will go and do the things which the Lord hath commanded, for I know that the Lord giveth no commandments unto the children of men, save he shall prepare a way for them that they may accomplish the thing which he commandeth them.

Sonnet 357 1 Nephi 3:7

We speak of testimony from the start
Expressions of belief are shared in love
And simple faith from deep within the heart
Is poured out like the sunshine from above.

And then when pure belief is on display
I ask a simple question with a smile
"Will you accept a call?" is all I say
And quick there comes the answer without guile.

So many Nephis in the church today!
Who never think to murmur or protest
Who think of nothing else but to obey.
And answer "Yes!" before they hear the test.

I hope that I'm the sort, when called, who stands
And goes and does whatever God commands.

Sonnet 498 1 Nephi 3:7 (#2)

It can't be fun to do as Nephi did
Oh sure we envy faith like his a lot
But we don't line up for his type of bid
What he is selling isn't often bought.

We buy instead the line that others sell
The one that says we have to think ahead
And only do what common sense will tell
Be safe, be sure, plan every step you tread.

All Nephi had to work with was his trust
Not knowing in advance the how or when
That God upon declaring what he must
Had done the preparation for his win.

Yeah, that can't be much fun. And stressful too!
I'll stick with doing things the way I do.

2 Nephi 2:25 Adam fell that men might be; and men are, that they might have joy.

Sonnet 532 2 Nephi 2:25

When Adam fell the devil danced with joy
His mission, so he thought, was on its way
And more than just to bother and annoy
He guessed he'd put all heaven in delay.

Yes he supposed he'd pile his misery
Unfettered upon Adam's hapless sons
And watch them lose their hard won liberty
Like all his first estate devoted ones.

He should have understood, as others did,
That falling opened up the way for man
To come to earth and make a precious bid
To put in practice heaven's happy plan.

So his was not a joy to last at all
Twas rather ours to be from Adam's fall.

2 Nephi 2:27 Wherefore, men are free according to the flesh; and all things are given them which are expedient unto man. And they are free to choose liberty and eternal life, through the great Mediator of all men, or to choose captivity and death, according to the captivity and power of the devil; for he seeketh that all men might be miserable like unto himself.

Sonnet 534 2 Nephi 2: 27

I take my table at this house of pain
And study such a menu as I can
The choices range from sacred to profane
To tempt the every appetite of man.

It all looks very good, at my first glance
But then I cast my eyes towards the price
Each item's cost is shown in advance
Precise, clear-cut, exactly and concise.

To those who focus on the end result
The meal is chosen easily that's best
No need to worry study or consult
Ignore the false descriptions, now undressed.

And so I order up, and catch my breath
I've chose between eternal life and death!

2 Nephi 9:28-29
28 O that cunning plan of the evil one! O the vainness, and the frailties, and the foolishness of men! When they are learned they think they are wise, and they hearken not unto the counsel of God, for they set it aside, supposing they know of themselves, wherefore, their wisdom is foolishness and it profiteth them not. And they shall perish.
29 But to be learned is good if they hearken unto the counsels of God.

Sonnet 568 2 Nephi 9:28-29

We hear of those who know of just enough
To to themselves and others danger bring
Or put another way, we sometimes bluff
A little knowledge is a dangerous thing.

But if a little can be bad, it seems
A lot of knowledge may be even worse
As such a learned person in their dreams
Is prone to bring upon themselves a curse.

They tend, in vanity to thus confuse
How wisdom differs from the learning curve
And end up caught up in the age old ruse
That they are smarter than the God they serve.

Thus giving counsel to the God of light
Is certain proof that someone's not too bright.

Sonnet 569 2 Nephi 9:28-29 (#2)

Unless they take a bearing from the sun
Or stars or even far off mounts or trees
Their balance being critically undone
The lost will simply circle in the breeze.

And while the fit and hardy make good time
And cover much more ground than those less trained
If they're just turning circles on their climb
There's nothing by this fitness to be gained.

However, much of good is magnified
When fitness and obedience collude
A prospect true but very seldom tried
Since vanity is bred by aptitude.

Remember if you want to stay on track
Keep counsel so you never circle back.

2 Nephi 25:23,26
23 For we labor diligently to write, to persuade our children, and also our brethren, to believe in Christ, and to be reconciled to God; for we know that it is by grace that we are saved, after all we can do.
26 And we talk of Christ, we rejoice in Christ, we preach of Christ, we prophesy of Christ, and we write according to our prophecies, that our children may know to what source they may look for a remission of their sins.

Sonnet 506 2 Nephi 25: 23, 26

We sometimes play a game of hide and seek
Or scavenge hunt for objects just for fun
Or share the secrets of Nimrod's technique
In deer camp while we polish up our gun.

Also we tease our children to pursue
Things lost. To learn the joy of what's found.
And have the faith and confidence anew
To search for truth where counterfeits abound.

But do not be deceived or fail to note
Your child will sometime feel he's lost... depressed
His sin will bring eternal loss of hope
Unless he knows the source of peace and rest.

So if your children will avoid torment
They must be taught, by you, how to repent.

Sonnet 715 2 Nephi 25: 23, 26 (#2)

Those little listening ears can hear it all
They're learning, leaning, sifting what we say
And even as they're testing out their crawl
Absorbing verbal clues is child's play.

And what do these, our infants, hear from us?
Complaints? Concerns? Corrections? All our cares?
Or prattle, gossip, idle talk and fuss?
Our focus will most likely become theirs.

And what do we record for future eyes
What will our great great grandkids find of use
If they explore our blog or journal tries
Will they find mostly just our daily blues?

But those who often write and speak of Christ
Deliver pearls of wisdom greatly priced.

2 Nephi 28:7-9 **7 Yea, and there shall be many which shall say: Eat, drink, and be merry, for tomorrow we die; and it shall be well with us.**

8 And there shall also be many which shall say: Eat, drink, and be merry; nevertheless, fear God—he will justify in committing a little sin; yea, lie a little, take the advantage of one because of his words, dig a pit for thy neighbor; there is no harm in this; and do all these things, for tomorrow we die; and if it so be that we are guilty, God will beat us with a few stripes, and at last we shall be saved in the kingdom of God.

9 Yea, and there shall be many which shall teach after this manner, false and vain and foolish doctrines, and shall be puffed up in their hearts, and shall seek deep to hide their counsels from the Lord; and their works shall be in the dark.

Sonnet 716 2 Nephi 28:7-9

Instead of overeating we might fast
Instead of drinking we should turn to prayer
And making merry isn't going to last
Obedience should be our first affair.

Remember we were set apart for more
For higher things than "party all the time"
We need to be a comfort to the poor
And nothing ever justifies a crime.

Don't buy the line that we can mess up now
Just have our fun and later see the light
Sow wild oats and then repent somehow
Such doctrine is the darkest of the night.

The purpose of this life is to prepare
Not party til you're caught in Satan's snare.

2 Nephi 31:19-20
19 And now, my beloved brethren, after ye have gotten into this strait and narrow path, I would ask if all is done? Behold, I say unto you, Nay; for ye have not come thus far save it were by the word of Christ with unshaken faith in him, relying wholly upon the merits of him who is mighty to save.
20 Wherefore, ye must press forward with a steadfastness in Christ, having a perfect brightness of hope, and a love of God and of all men. Wherefore, if ye shall press forward, feasting upon the word of Christ, and endure to the end, behold, thus saith the Father: Ye shall have eternal life.

Sonnet 717 2 Nephi 31:10-20

From time to time we feel the Spirit's touch
And get enthused about the holy writ
We read, we ponder, and make notes and such
But other times, I guess, we just forget.

And sometimes we are full of honest hope
We see the light and joyfully submit
We pray, we serve, we have eternal scope
But other times, I guess, we just forget.

And sometimes we have love for God and man
Our hearts with everyone seem firmly knit
We give, we share, we do more than we can
But other times, I guess, we just forget.

We have to make remembering a trend
That's what we call enduring to the end.

2 Nephi 32:3
 3 Angels speak by the power of the Holy Ghost; wherefore, they speak the words of Christ. Wherefore, I said unto you, feast upon the words of Christ; for behold, the words of Christ will tell you all things what ye should do.

Sonnet 718 2 Nephi 32:3

You don't need special guidance to be good
The path of gospel living's easy found
There isn't much to be misunderstood
Just do what's right and never mess around.

But you have something greater to become
There's valiant epic missions to be mined
And heights and depths of sacrifice to plumb
Potential that you need to search and find.

For that you have to feast, to fast, to pray
To study and to listen and in fact
To ponder and to hearken and obey
And as you see your way, you need to act.

Imagine how much can be made of you
If Christ has told you all things you should do.

2 Nephi 32:8-9

8 And now, my beloved brethren, I perceive that ye ponder still in your hearts; and it grieveth me that I must speak concerning this thing. For if ye would hearken unto the Spirit which teacheth a man to pray, ye would know that ye must pray; for the evil spirit teacheth not a man to pray, but teacheth him that he must not pray.

9 But behold, I say unto you that ye must pray always, and not faint; that ye must not perform any thing unto the Lord save in the first place ye shall pray unto the Father in the name of Christ, that he will consecrate thy performance unto thee, that thy performance may be for the welfare of thy soul.

Sonnet 719 2 Nephi 32:8-9

The devil doesn't love or even care
He doesn't wish you happiness or well
His misery is all he wants to share
Well, that and all the wretchedness in hell.

But God declares and demonstrates His love
His mission is to give eternal life
To qualify you for a home above.
And lift you up to joy and out of strife.

And all you have to do is make a choice
Expressed perhaps in this the simplest way
By giving an affirmatory voice
In answer to the question - Will you pray?

And if your answer's no, or even faint
You set yourself a course of sure complaint.

Mosiah 2:17
17 And behold, I tell you these things that ye may learn wisdom; that ye may learn that when ye are in the service of your fellow beings ye are only in the service of your God.

Sonnet 720 Mosiah 2:17

There is no better tonic for your health
No better medicine or drug or cure
It's better than the benefits of wealth
It's sanctifying strengthening and pure.

There is no smarter way to carry on
No plan of life that beats or matches it
No building up of muscles or of brawn
That gives a fraction of its benefit.

And it's a constant source of love and joy
The happiness and kindness that it brings
The banishment of things that might annoy
Without it nothing smiles, delights or sings.

Through selfless service of your fellow man
You take an honoured place in heaven's plan.

Mosiah 3:19
For the natural man is an enemy to God, and has been from the fall of Adam, and will be, forever and ever, unless he yields to the enticings of the Holy Spirit, and putteth off the natural man and becometh a saint through the atonement of Christ the Lord, and becometh as a child, submissive, meek, humble, patient, full of love, willing to submit to all things which the Lord seeth fit to inflict upon him, even as a child doth submit to his father.

Sonnet 493 Mosiah 3:19

Who wants the artificial anymore?
Promotions of what's natural are bold
Just look around in any grocery store
It's natural that cries out to be sold.

And in our "feels good" value sort of way
We laud the basest instincts of the man
No talk of rising up above that fray
We hunker down, accepting any plan.

But God would have us reach a new plateau
Not artificial, but more real by far
Put off the ordinary and the low
And climb above your nature, to a star.

And how to climb is irony supreme
Put on his easy yoke and find your dream.

Mosiah 4:30
But this much I can tell you, that if ye do not watch yourselves, and your thoughts, and your words, and your deeds, and observe the commandments of God, and continue in the faith of what ye have heard concerning the coming of our Lord, even unto the end of your lives, ye must perish. And now, O man, remember, and perish not.

Sonnet 495 Reflections on Mosiah 4:30

Some principles have proxies in the writ
Alternative or stand-in words that point
To something more important than the bit
Of meaning that the words themselves anoint.

To show it, here's a test you ought to try
Replace a word with something else and see
If meanings are unlocked when you apply
The proxy to the passage as a key.

Now where you read "remember" say "repent"
Then think if that expands the verse's aim
And next, see if it adds to what is meant
If you give "watch yourselves" the same new name.

First principles are rife with proxy friends
The scripture student's magnifying lens.

Alma 7:11-13 11 And he shall go forth, suffering pains and afflictions and temptations of every kind; and this that the word might be fulfilled which saith he will take upon him the pains and the sicknesses of his people.

12 And he will take upon him death, that he may loose the bands of death which bind his people; and he will take upon him their infirmities, that his bowels may be filled with mercy, according to the flesh, that he may know according to the flesh how to succor his people according to their infirmities.

13 Now the Spirit knoweth all things; nevertheless the Son of God suffereth according to the flesh that he might take upon him the sins of his people, that he might blot out their transgressions according to the power of his deliverance; and now behold, this is the testimony which is in me.

Sonnet 721 Alma 7:11-13

The things we're powerless alone to win
We classify as deficits this way
First there's the awful awkwardness of sin
Then death and lastly sickness and dismay.

These three the consequences of the fall
Inflicted as afflictions for a cause
To turn us to the Savior of us all
As we embrace His mercy and His laws.

Atoning for the painful path of sin
Arising from the grasping grip of death
And lifting life's extremities therein
The Savior beckons us with every breath.

Our freedom and this absence and our pain
Were all planned out for our eternal gain.

Sonnet 722 Alma 7:11-13 (#2)

Remember in that board game played with dice
That when in jail you have to roll this way
A seven or eleven or a twice
To move beyond the prison of the day.

So think of that whenever in a bind
The double could be Alma one and two
Then seven and eleven bring to mind
So this citation sticks in mind for you.

Remember. Oh remember as you must
The ways atoning sacrifice can save
Don't ever be forgetful of its thrust
Much more than just redemption and the grave.

Bring all your sickness, sadness and your pains
And Christ will also loose you from those chains.

Alma 32:21
21 And now as I said concerning faith—faith is not to have a perfect knowledge of things; therefore if ye have faith ye hope for things which are not seen, which are true.

Sonnet 723 Alma 32:21

Some people put their faith in Powerball
Or Lotto 649 or slots or cards
While others can't resist a sirens call
Their virtue sold in hope of cheap rewards.

Still others hope that work will work for them
They toil and they moil and they dig
They hope to find in daily grind their gem
Through bank accounts and houses that are big.

And some require approval of the crowd
Or look for drugs or booze to bring their joys
Or stake their faith and hopes in being proud
Ironically embracing what destroys.

We show our hope and faith by what we do
The trick is to have faith in what is true.

Alma 37:35
35 O, remember, my son, and learn wisdom in thy youth; yea, learn in thy youth to keep the commandments of God.

Sonnet 724 Alma 37:35

Sea captains need an anchor they can trust
In worship there's no substitute for prayer
In building, firm foundations are a must
And working from a corner stone that's square.

In navigation it's the polar star
That fixed and constant point of stellar light
Since finding heaven shows us where we are
And keeps the safe and peaceful path in sight.

And everyone needs principles and truth
To fix and bathe their way with guiding light
And even in the blossoming of youth
The wise will learn to seek for what is right.

And wisdom of the ages shows to me
That keeping the commandments is the key.

Alma 39:9
9 Now my son, I would that ye should repent and forsake your sins, and go no more after the lusts of your eyes, but cross yourself in all these things; for except ye do this ye can in nowise inherit the kingdom of God. Oh, remember, and take it upon you, and cross yourself in these things.

Sonnet 725 Alma 39:9

Sometimes a common theme is best described
In words uncommon to the listening ear
At first you ask yourself just what's transcribed
But with some effort meanings become clear.

To cross yourself may sound so thusly strange
But here is what this father really meant
To turn, regret, to overcome, to change
Uncommon for the common term repent.

Some things we think or do need crossing out
Because, in fact, they sadly cross the line
Or cut across our faith and into doubt
And so we cross ourselves to realign.

But let's not lose what gives this verse its clout
We all have things to cross ourselves about.

Alma 41:10
10 Do not suppose, because it has been spoken concerning restoration, that ye shall be restored from sin to happiness. Behold, I say unto you, wickedness never was happiness.

Sonnet 726 Alma 41:10

While resurrection patches up some things
Like blindness or a limp or lack of hair
The things that sinful wicked living brings
The simple act of dying can't repair.

That happiness you thought might come from sin
The peace of mind that guilty pleasures spoil
That joy reduced by error to chagrin
Will not be found by shuffling off this coil.

Repentance works its magic now and here
Its cleansing is designed for this estate
Don't let it's easy access disappear
By putting off the clean up till too late.

I hope I never hear this harsh demand
What part of "never" don't you understand?

Helaman 5:12
And now, my sons, remember, remember that it is upon the rock of our Redeemer, who is Christ, the Son of God, that ye must build your foundation; that when the devil shall send forth his mighty winds, yea, his shafts in the whirlwind, yea, when all his hail and his mighty storm shall beat upon you, it shall have no power over you to drag you down to the gulf of misery and endless wo, because of the rock upon which ye are built, which is a sure foundation, a foundation whereon if men build they cannot fall.

Sonnet 489 Helaman 5:12

There is no place on earth to build that's right
To beat the power of wind and wave and storm
No mix of man-made concrete has the might
To save against what nature can perform.

And even sun and water wear out stone
And granite mountains wash away at last
This world cannot be permanency prone
With so much vigour in destructive blast.

And molten white hot lava at the core
Unstable as the water in the foam
That beats against the ocean's ragged shore
Is threat'ning any time to melt this home.

Don't build your dreams upon this earthy tent
Foundations that endure are heaven sent.

3 Nephi 12:48
48 Therefore I would that ye should be perfect even as I, or your Father who is in heaven is perfect.

Sonnet 727 3 Nephi 12:48A

A perfect baby cannot even walk
Or understand the consequence of sin
And needs some time to learn to even talk
Before much education can begin.

A perfect child is still in need of aid
Will say and do the very darndest things
His state of immaturity displayed
In what most every daily challenge brings.

A perfect adult now begins to learn
The ways of virtue, patience and of love
To pray and bridle passions and to turn
For comfort and for guidance from above.

While perfect gods are free from all mistakes
The perfect man repents from those he makes.

3 Nephi 18:15,20-21

15 Verily, verily, I say unto you, ye must watch and pray always, lest ye be tempted by the devil, and ye be led away captive by him.

20 And whatsoever ye shall ask the Father in my name, which is right, believing that ye shall receive, behold it shall be given unto you.

21 Pray in your families unto the Father, always in my name, that your wives and your children may be blessed.

Sonnet 728 3 Nephi 18:15,20-21
It's hard to be on duty all the time
To be on watch, on sentry or on call
Your focus fixed upon all things sublime
Attentive to all threats, however small.

The simple way to check your vigilance
To gauge how guarded and alert you are
Is taking counsel from Omnipotence
By making prayer your constant guiding star.

And there are watchmen on the towers too
Who issue warnings of the next assault
It pays to take advantage of their view
And watch and heed those watchers to a fault.

The devil's out to steal your soul away
Remember then to always watch and pray.

Ether 12:6
6 And now, I, Moroni, would speak somewhat concerning these things; I would show unto the world that faith is things which are hoped for and not seen; wherefore, dispute not because ye see not, for ye receive no witness until after the trial of your faith.

Sonnet 729 Ether 12:6

It's not that there's no evidence for it
All things, we're told, denote that God is real
It's just that faith's a future sort of fit
We use it now, then wait for the "reveal".

We have the testimonies of the past
These records by the gift and power of God
And even current light is widely cast
To show the fear of darkness as a fraud.

So though our faith is tested in a way
Because we cannot see beyond our light
The simple facts are really plain as day
With faith, there cannot be an actual night.

Come on! Don't waste your time in blind debate
The witness and the miracle await.

Ether 12:27
27 And if men come unto me I will show unto them their weakness. I give unto men weakness that they may be humble; and my grace is sufficient for all men that humble themselves before me; for if they humble themselves before me, and have faith in me, then will I make weak things become strong unto them.

Sonnet 730 Ether 12:27

A farmer who will not look out for weeds
Is likely to have trouble in his fields
And even if he plants all healthy seeds
There will be disappointment in his yields.

The greatest sin and curse of life is pride
Because the prideful will not see their faults
And thus without perspective they're denied
The perfect way to better their results.

To understand the nature of their plight
The wise and humble of the earth will seek
To fix the things that are not going right
By firstly finding out just where they're weak.

So come to Christ and He will make you strong
By showing you just where you're weak and wrong.

Moroni 7:41

41 And what is it that ye shall hope for? Behold I say unto you that ye shall have hope through the atonement of Christ and the power of his resurrection, to be raised unto life eternal, and this because of your faith in him according to the promise.

Sonnet 731 Moroni 7:41

We line up for a ticket or a chance
We crowd to get to where the dice are thrown
We pull upon the handle in a trance
True reasons for this madness left unknown.

If questioned we will give the story thus
"We do it for the thrill and for the fun,
It's harmless entertainment – why the fuss?"
And then continue gambling 'til we're done.

We do not seem to understand what makes
Us play until we've been completely skinned
What inner craving falsely by this takes
Our common sense and throws it to the wind?

If we reject the only hope that's true
Some vain and foolish hope will have to do.

Moroni 7:45, 47-48 45 And charity suffereth long, and is kind, and envieth not, and is not puffed up, seeketh not her own, is not easily provoked, thinketh no evil, and rejoiceth not in iniquity but rejoiceth in the truth, beareth all things, believeth all things, hopeth all things, endureth all things.
 47 But charity is the pure love of Christ, and it endureth forever; and whoso is found possessed of it at the last day, it shall be well with him.
 48 Wherefore, my beloved brethren, pray unto the Father with all the energy of heart, that ye may be filled with this love, which he hath bestowed upon all who are true followers of his Son, Jesus Christ; that ye may become the sons of God; that when he shall appear we shall be like him, for we shall see him as he is; that we may have this hope; that we may be purified even as he is pure. Amen.

Sonnet 732 Moroni 7:45;47-48

This Christ-like love is quite a bit to bear
You cannot keep your favourites that way
You'll have to dine with publicans and share
The suffering of every man's dismay.

You'll have to learn and try the healer's art
You'll work to set the sinful captive free
The poor and hungry will invade your heart
You'll tell the stranger "Come and follow me."

And then your loaves and fishes will increase
Your insufficient talents will suffice
And you will find a deep unworldly peace
A pure enduring pearl without price.

This love that only comes through heartfelt prayer
Is worth whatever cost you have to bear.

Moroni 10:4-5
4 And when ye shall receive these things, I would exhort you that ye would ask God, the Eternal Father, in the name of Christ, if these things are not true; and if ye shall ask with a sincere heart, with real intent, having faith in Christ, he will manifest the truth of it unto you, by the power of the Holy Ghost.
5 And by the power of the Holy Ghost ye may know the truth of all things.

Sonnet 508 Moroni 10:4-5

When baking something wonderful and sweet
Like bread or cake or pie or quiche or tart
The recipe for such a pleasant treat
Requires attention to its every part.

You won't get far if features are left out
(A bread without its leavening won't rise)
And so the baker wisely is devout
To every step the recipe applies.

And recipes for following truth's way
Must be a code worth more than any bread
And more important therefore to obey
The rules that lead to such a golden thread.

So ponder each instruction in this verse
The most important recipe on earth.

Doctrine and Covenants

D&C 1:37-38
37 Search these commandments, for they are true and faithful, and the prophecies and promises which are in them shall all be fulfilled.
38 What I the Lord have spoken, I have spoken, and I excuse not myself; and though the heavens and the earth pass away, my word shall not pass away, but shall all be fulfilled, whether by mine own voice or by the voice of my servants, it is the same.

Sonnet 775 D&C 1:37-38

I give my cheers of gratitude and love
A grand Hurrah! And happy hoot Hooray!
Then Hallelujah! To my God above
Hosanna! For this restoration day.

My shout is meant to come from deep within
And spread, I hope, across the universe
The message of respite from death and sin
Commandments overcoming Satan's curse.

And ordinances and the promised law
And prophesies and blessings and the word
Chastisement mixed with wisdom without flaw
The doctrine by its covenants conferred.

Hosanna! For this book of prophesy
And Hallelujah from a bended knee!

Sonnet 776 D&C 1:37-38 #2

Oh yes, the hunt is on. The search for truth
For wisdom of the open public kind
And mysteries demanding more the sleuth
The plain and precious and the hard to find.

And here's the promised place to win that search
A guarantee of finding all your needs
The scripture that designed the Savior's Church
A guiding light for anyone that reads.

So hardly could you find a better place
In which to search for clues for living right
This latter-day description of His grace
The modern Way of Truth and Life and Light.

These true and faithful covenants for you
And doctrine, promises, commandments too.

Sonnet 776 D&C 1:37-38 #3

The precious word of God. Eternal! True!
Restoring all the ways ordained at first
Outlasting earth and heaven, and yet new
An everlasting covenant now versed.

Declaring boldly that the prophets' tongue
Is equal and a proxy for His own
The unison of God and prophet sung
Identical in meaning and in tone.

If you would keep the first and great command
To love your God with all your heart and might
You must apply your mind to understand
His Word and make its practice your delight.

And never without casting out the King
Can you discount the words His servants bring.

D&C 6:36
36 Look unto me in every thought; doubt not, fear not.

Sonnet 777 D&C 6:36

I'm not sure how this works if one is blind
But for the sighted, something one should know
The looker, in the end, is sure to find
That where he looks is where he tends to go.

Of course this can be good or bad for him
Depending on the focus of his sight
An evil seeker's future will be grim
A righteous looker's prospects will be bright.

And there is much distraction out there too
Carcinogens dress up to look benign
The competition for your point of view
Began as soon as earth was in design.

So watch the things you watch my sighted friend
Remember, where you look is where you'll end.

Sonnet 778 D&C 6:36 #2

Some people train a horse with seeming ease
Or show old dogs the workings of new tricks
A few can even teach a cat to please
Or make a circus out of fleas and ticks.

And others, well they like to train their hair
Or build their bodies into muscle shows
They do it with astounding time and care
And why they do it no one really knows.

But did you ever think to train your thoughts
To make them servant to your needs and wants
Not letting them run loose or tie in knots
Or settle in their own unhealthy haunts?

We're told to look to God in every thought
I think about that challenge quite a lot.

Sonnet 779 D&C 6:36 #3

You may protest that such a bold command
As that to tell you not to fear or doubt
Defies the normal way we understand
That feelings such as these can turn about.

We tend to think we're powerless to change
The course of unbelief or faith or love
That fate or circumstances will arrange
And we the victims more or less thereof.

But if the Lord commands us to believe
And tells us not to fear or faint or doubt
Then clearly that's a thread that we can weave
An outcome in our pow'r to bring about.

And in this verse the pattern is explained
Control your thoughts and faith will be sustained.

D&C 8:2-3

2 Yea, behold, I will tell you in your mind and in your heart, by the Holy Ghost, which shall come upon you and which shall dwell in your heart.

3 Now, behold, this is the spirit of revelation; behold, this is the spirit by which Moses brought the children of Israel through the Red Sea on dry ground.

Sonnet 780 D&C 8:2-3

If you can Skype a cousin in L.A.
Or phone or Facetime someone further still
If you can click and speed along its way
A message of intention or good will.

If you can play on-line what's all the rage
Or tweet your every move throughout the day
And make and keep a friendly Facebook page
Or buy and play a song the iTunes way.

If you can feel the music of a Bach
Or ponder on the life of Socrates
Or sculpt a figure from a marble block
Or taste the miracle that comes from bees.

All this without much knowing on your part
Then why can't God speak to your mind and heart?

Sonnet 781 D&C 8:2-3 #2

There is a battle royal in your chest
Of forces which would dwell within your heart
And that which you would want to nourish best
Will have the chance to occupy that part.

You furnish and equip that dwelling spot
According as your choices have matured
By your profane or by your holy thought
The comfort of your tenant is assured.

So think about your life in just this way -
What sort of guest does my heart best accord
Is what I think and say and do each day
Inviting to the devil – or the Lord?

And is it time to renovate your suite
And build a much more spiritual retreat?

Sonnet 782 D&C 8:2-3 #3

In every life there's moments of despair
When enemies assail and close the way
When hardship becomes more than you can bear
And all seems lost and hope is in decay.

And backed up to the water of the sea
Was Moses and his people in retreat
And seeing that they could not fight or flee
They agonized and murmured in defeat.

But Moses had this special power to save
The gift of revelation from the Lord
To see a way to pass through any wave
A Word much stronger than the strongest sword.

So when in seas of trouble you seem drowned
The Spirit's there to help you find dry ground.

D&C 10:5
5 Pray always, that you may come off conqueror; yea, that you may conquer Satan, and that you may escape the hands of the servants of Satan that do uphold his work.

Sonnet 783 D&C 10:5

Those grasping hands of demon devotees
Commanded by a devil without heart
Can be defeated if you make your knees
The place on which your days will end and start.

And praying is a shield and weapon too
Against the evil forces of the day
For nothing has a chance to conquer you
If you will make the time to always pray.

You cannot pray a lie. As Huck would say
And so the truth will fortify the saint
And set you free as Christ explained the way
That we ought always pray and not to faint.

Since how to conquer is so clearly said
You wonder why the losing's so widespread?

Sonnet 784 D&C 10:5 #2

I testify of music as a prayer
The holiness of melody that's strong
The remedy for darkness or despair
I praise the healing and the gift of song.

I sing of earth and heaven and of life
I cast out fear with lovely lullabies
I charge the battle front with drum and fife
And every song's a prayer, a sign, a prize.

I join the chorus in triumphant airs
Or make a joyful noise within my heart
Delighting in my choice of tuneful prayers
I worship with my voice as blessed art.

And this is how I conquer Satan's force
With happy sacred music as my course.

D&C 13:1
1 Upon you my fellow servants, in the name of Messiah I confer the Priesthood of Aaron, which holds the keys of the ministering of angels, and of the gospel of repentance, and of baptism by immersion for the remission of sins; and this shall never be taken again from the earth, until the sons of Levi do offer again an offering unto the Lord in righteousness.

Sonnet 785: D&C 13:1

Imagine if you will the thrill of this
Of John the Baptist calling you by name
And if, in such a moment of pure bliss
"My fellow servant" did he too exclaim.

My habit, with a similar address
Is to begin with "We your brethren lay
Our hands upon your head" to lift and bless
And keys, a call or comfort thus convey.

The fellowship of saints is first and last
The unity and love and friendship must
In deed and every word be kindly passed
Acknowledging the order of the just.

And even here between the dispensations
Some words to show the parity of stations.

Sonnet 786 D&C 13:1 #2

The order and the genius of these rights
That give a place of service to the young
Preparing for the necessary heights
Allowing upward progress rung by rung.

This priesthood is important needed power
And every holder ought to comprehend
Though higher office should begin to flower
He's still a deacon to the very end.

It can't be small to hold the angel's keys
To minister to basic needs of men
To turn them from uncaring to their knees
Ensuring that the sinner's born again.

I hope, for me, these duties never wain
Just cause the sons of Levi come again.

Sonnet 787 D&C 13:1 #3

Moroni held the keys to prove the cause
And so he laid the word at Joseph's door
A gift that put an end to the long pause
According to all prophesy before.

And so as Joseph had the proof in hand
The power next conferred upon his head
As angels came as needed to expand
The keys to govern how this work would spread.

These visits from iconic ancient men
Elijah, Moses, Michael, Peter too
And James and Johns and Gabriel and then
Some other angels that we never knew.

So with the word, the power and the keys
The Gospel now restored will spread with ease.

D&C 18:10-11
10 Remember the worth of souls is great in the sight of God;
12 For, behold, the Lord your Redeemer suffered death in the flesh; wherefore he suffered the pain of all men, that all men might repent and come unto him.

Sonnet 788 D&C 18:10-11

The Scottish poet begs to have the gift
To see ourselves as others see us too
And while that might provide a social lift
Far better to see me as God sees you.

The issue here is clarity of sight
Of recognizing value where it lies
In overcoming tendency to slight
The value seen so clearly by God's eyes.

And even when we see the worth of souls
We later on forget just what we've seen
Confused by all our lesser mortal goals
Forgetting who we are and where we've been.

To help remember, singing's what I do
"I Am a Child of God". And so are you.

Sonnet 789 D&C 18:10-11 #2

To know the value of most any thing
A guess, a wish, or hope will not suffice
And even an appraisal has a swing
So great it only sets an asking price.

And tougher yet to cost out souls on earth
No catalogue of these is found in play
And so, as with the things, the person's worth
Is only set by how much one will pay.

But here a final price point has been set
A payment that is infinite and firm
Retirement of all of mankind's debt
Atonement made completely and full term.

There is no pain, no loss, no fault or sin
That Christ cannot redeem. Just come to Him.

D&C 18:15-16

15 And if it so be that you should labor all your days in crying repentance unto this people, and bring, save it be one soul unto me, how great shall be your joy with him in the kingdom of my Father!

16 And now, if your joy will be great with one soul that you have brought unto me into the kingdom of my Father, how great will be your joy if you should bring many souls unto me!

Sonnet 790 D&C 18:15-16

It's too late now for me to meet this test
I've spent too many days in sheer neglect
I haven't always tried my very best
My missionary zeal has been suspect.

But even in my accidental ways
I've stumbled to success a time or two
And tasted of this joy in my days
By doing what good missionaries do.

And much as anyone who should repent
I need to keep in mind these joys I've had
And over come the forces that prevent
Me from pursing things that make me glad.

I guess if I would "labour all my days"
I'll have to start today to change my ways.

Sonnet 791 D&C 18 15-16 #2

Just yesterday a flicker of this light
As I was working in my temple role
A patron sitting, smiling, to my right
A lovely, worthy, happy, favoured soul.

Reminded of a blessing from the past
I knew her from my seminary days
She came, a stranger, yearning, learning fast
And left a member, baptized in our ways.

Between the sealings I called out her name
And she, "My seminary teacher. Hey!"
And then, "My favourite student!" I exclaim
A joyful moment brightening the day.

Reunions up in heaven much like this
Will surely be the stuff of heavenly bliss.

Sonnet 792 D&C 18: 15-16 #3

And some may labour all their days, I fear
And never see, in life, the joyfulness
Of bringing even one soul to or near
The Holy One who wants to own and bless.

Some even serve a mission for two years
And knock on doors and cry repentance loud
And overcome temptation and their fears
And yet can't pick a convert from the crowd.

And seeing others easily succeed
Can't help but be discouraging to such
Who, giving all they can, still humbly plead
For someone, somewhere, sometime they can touch.

That saint, in joy, will have a great reward
For having brought his own soul to the Lord.

D&C 19:16-19
16 For behold, I, God, have suffered these things for all, that they might not suffer if they would repent;
17 But if they would not repent they must suffer even as I;
18 Which suffering caused myself, even God, the greatest of all, to tremble because of pain, and to bleed at every pore, and to suffer both body and spirit—and would that I might not drink the bitter cup, and shrink—
19 Nevertheless, glory be to the Father, and I partook and finished my preparations unto the children of men.

Sonnet 793 D&C 19:16-19

Because there is no happiness in sin
And since the fall temptation came about
We all know some of misery within
And even some of suffering without.

And with this understanding comes the need
To lift the consequences from the soul
Erasing every evil thought and deed
To meet eternity both clean and whole.

And so a loving Father, God and King
Decreed a plan for ending all such pains
It called for someone else to bear the sting
Of all the awful hurt that sin sustains.

Because the Savior drank that bitter cup
Each fallen sinner can be lifted up.

Sonnet 794 D&C 19:16-19 #2

The Lord must really love a metaphor
In allegory, irony and such
He teaches us with parables galore
To give His doctrine lessons, common touch.

And here He teaches with the bitter cup
Remember, upper room, where first He gave
His loving friends the charge to drink it up
And then Gethsemane. The cup. The save.

And finally upon the awful cross
In irony triumphant did he cry
For having paid the full and awful cost
"I thirst" from having drunk the bitter dry.

And every week the cup is passed to you
Reminding of a debt that's always due.

D&C 19:23
23 Learn of me, and listen to my words; walk in the meekness of my Spirit, and you shall have peace in me.

Sonnet 795 D&C 19:23

And here's that threesome counsel yet again
Three things to do to earn a promise true
It's learn, and listen, walk in meekness, then
The peace of God will come, with Him, to you.

As usual these three duties are not new
They represent a very common theme
As "study", "pray" and "work", is what we do
To keep our daily progress on the beam.

Don't let a day go by without a touch
Of learning of the word in holy writ
And no one ever listened overmuch
So praying always is a benefit.

And, thirdly, work should be your daily walk
No meekness ever grew just out of talk.

Sonnet 796 D&C 19:23 #2

The Lord hath said it well and truly so
There is no peace unto the wicked souls
No rest, no sweet refreshment where they go
No rescue from their wrecks on wretched shoals.

The peace and safety promised is to penitent
Contrite and broken hearted lowly sons
And daughters who accept the heaven sent
Forgiveness promised to all humble ones.

There is no peace unless you're right with God
Obedient and diligent and good
Unless you learn to worship and applaud
The gospel message rightly understood.

So learning, listening and walking true
Is what you do to bring His peace to you.

D&C 25:13
13 Wherefore, lift up thy heart and rejoice, and cleave unto the covenants which thou hast made.

Sonnet 797 D&C 25:13

A life without a covenant is vain
Without a promise solemn made and kept
A life without commitment is profane
A waste, a loss, it's squandered and inept.

But covenants with God give life it's zest
A reach for something higher than your own
The way to rise triumphant in the test
A purpose and a sceptre and a throne.

So cleave unto your covenants with zeal
Rejoice to have great meaning and the means
To guide your heart and soul with such a keel
Against the winds of chance and change of scenes.

A kite can never fly without a string
And that's the sort of power that covenants bring.

Sonnet 798 D&C 25:13 #2

What habit could be better than this one
To lift your heart, rejoice and be glad
For all the things the Lord for you has done
A tonic to dispel what's sad or bad.

Today may disappoint or set you back
A lot of things may seem to go all wrong
But joyfulness will keep you on the track
So live your life as if it was a song.

Don't be so thoughtless of your blessed state
Remind yourself, instead, of promised peace
Impressions of depression will abate
When joyfulness begins and grumblings cease.

Rejoice, rejoice! Make that your daily choice
Rejoice, rejoice! Make that your daily voice.

D&C 46:33
33 And ye must practice virtue and holiness before me continually. Even so. Amen.

Sonnet 799 D&C 46:33

Most things take practice to improve at all
The skills in others we admire so
Do not appear by simple beck and call
But rather by the force of practice grow.

Perhaps to play piano or the flute
And make pure melodies through constant care
Is not so diff'rent from the special route
That leads to virtue, holiness and prayer.

The Savior of the world even grew
And waxed strong in the spirit and was wise
Thus learning by the grace of God to do
The mighty works required to win His prize.

So pick a virtue, practice it, and tell
How holiness can grow when practised well.

Sonnet 800 D&C 46:33 #2

What are the constants in your daily walk
What habits are the measure of your way
What interests consume your idle talk
What marks the nature of your day to day?

Perhaps you have a love of lovely song
Or are you one to follow every game
Or is the workplace where you're really strong
Or do you seek for riches or for fame?

There's some who seem in trouble all the time
And others always focused on their looks
I s'pose there's some who toil away at rhyme
And others who do nothing but read books.

But if you must do anything a lot
Be sure that virtue occupies that spot.

D&C 58:27
27 Verily I say, men should be anxiously engaged in a good cause, and do many things of their own free will, and bring to pass much righteousness;

Sonnet 801 D&C 58:27

I see them every day, and it is sad
Those men engaged in things of little worth
Anxiety for causes small or bad
The champions of the trivial or worse.

Sincere, involved, concerned, enthused, caught up
They may attempt to recruit you as well
And similarly make your daily cup
No better than a porous empty shell.

Though all of us have some desires to build
Be not deceived. Large action in small things
Expends your force and makes you fill fulfilled
But nothing good or real or lasting brings.

So choose your cause with careful prayerful zeal
And make of your free will a first-rate deal.

Sonnet 802 D&C 58:27 #2

Of course there's much that's given by command
The line of proper action is defined
And covenants and callings can expand
Endeavours to which saints have been assigned.

And such as duty and command require
Is much and must be carefully observed
But do not think it takes your whole desire
There's other wants and wishes to be served.

The One who went about just doing good
Displayed the way to freelance your free will
So rise above just doing what you "should"
Let constant love of righteousness fulfill.

And be a better boy scout, just this way
By doing lots of good turns, everyday.

D&C 58:42-43
42 Behold, he who has repented of his sins, the same is forgiven, and I, the Lord, remember them no more.
43 By this ye may know if a man repenteth of his sins—behold, he will confess them and forsake them.

Sonnet 803 D&C 58:42-43

The miracles began and never quit
He turned some water into better wine
He made the blind to see with clay and spit
He cast demonic spirits into swine.

He woke the dead as if they were in sleep
For multitudes he multiplied their food
He walked across the waves above the deep
And at his word the tempests were subdued.

He put a severed ear back in its place
He withered barren fig trees at a glance
And healed a withered hand right in the face
Of Pharisees and scribes on Satan's dance.

Then finally, atonement, well and full
The gift of turning scarlet into wool.

Sonnet 804 D&C 58:42-43 #2

This business of repentance is the best
The ultimate in fashion and in style
The end of sins forsaken and confessed
Beats out all other blessings by a mile!

And how about a God who just forgets
Who takes you back to where you were before
Erases every aspect of regrets
And won't bring up the subject anymore!

Is there a pattern here for us to know
To blank out all offences, slights and wrongs
To move on, saddle up, and let it go
Forget the blues and sing more happy songs.

I hope the Christ-like virtue list's not set
I'd like to add a virtue: To forget.

D&C 64:9-11

9 Wherefore, I say unto you, that ye ought to forgive one another; for he that forgiveth not his brother his trespasses standeth condemned before the Lord; for there remaineth in him the greater sin.

10 I, the Lord, will forgive whom I will forgive, but of you it is required to forgive all men.

11 And ye ought to say in your hearts—let God judge between me and thee, and reward thee according to thy deeds.

Sonnet 805 D&C 64:9-11

When final judgment finally is wrought
I'll want for help and mercy to be sure
I'll need for sins forgiven and forgot
It takes a lot of grace to be judged pure.

And tragic would it be to have on hand
The silly sin of unforgivingness
The stupid simpleminded stubborn stand
That I should be the judge if you transgress.

Let God be judge of me, and more, of you
Forgive each brother freely and be free
Of such a mortal sin as wanting to
Be judge of those with whom we disagree.

I hope, for your sake, you've forgiven me
And that, for my sake, I've forgiven thee.

Sonnet 806 D&C 64:9-11 #2

The trespass may be grave or slight, who knows?
But somehow failing to forgive is worse
No matter how the first offence arose
The greater sin evokes a greater curse.

And while this seems a mystery at first
Unfair to victims innocent of guile
A second punishment to be disbursed
Upon the guiltless, yet another trial.

This simple fact in doctrine should be clear
Atonement makes account for every sin
And no one earns or bears the highest sphere
Until he leaves all judgments up to Him.

Since heaven is no place for keeping score
You need to check that baggage at the door.

D&C 76:22-24

22 And now, after the many testimonies which have been given of him, this is the testimony, last of all, which we give of him: That he lives!

23 For we saw him, even on the right hand of God; and we heard the voice bearing record that he is the Only Begotten of the Father—

24 That by him, and through him, and of him, the worlds are and were created, and the inhabitants thereof are begotten sons and daughters unto God.

Sonnet 490 D&C 76: 22-24

The voice I've heard is not the voice of man
But such as only heart and soul can feel
Yet stronger and more true than any plan
Devised to prove that something else is real.

And so because of this I know it's true
The testimony of this Joseph Smith
A declaration meant to best renew
The faith that Christ is not some ancient myth.

And since, the witnesses have multiplied
Until in millions saints affirm the Christ
And though they each have truly testified
Still, for the rest, it does not yet suffice.

Each must just ask to hear from Him that gives
The voice, at last, that testifies: He lives!

Sonnet 807 D&C 76:22-24 #2

This is the sort of evidence we use
In courts of law to sort out serious things
With solemn witnesses in threes or twos
The consequence of judgment swiftly brings.

You may believe, or not, it's up to you
Your agency allows you to decide
And even, once believing. What to do?
How should this testimony be applied?

Whatever you may choose to do, or not
On record now is evidence quite clear
This makes you bound, accountable and caught
You can't pretend there's nothing to see here.

I say, embrace the facts. The Savior lives!
What comfort this sweet testimony gives!

D&C 76:40-41
40 And this is the gospel, the glad tidings, which the voice out of the heavens bore record unto us—
41 That he came into the world, even Jesus, to be crucified for the world, and to bear the sins of the world, and to sanctify the world, and to cleanse it from all unrighteousness;

Sonnet 808 D&C 76:40-41

Each day I check the news to see what's new
I listen to the stories of the day
And weather, sports and things the nations do
I like to learn what's going on that way.

And most of what I hear is pretty mean
The troubles and the strife are what they sell
The crime, the plagues and even the obscene
Are all reported faithfully and well.

But there is always news that's always good
Glad tidings, new and ancient, always true
Although not in the nightly news, it should
Be something that I constantly review.

Between the nightly and the glad please choose
The Gospel as most valued piece of news.

Sonnet 808 D&C 76:40-41 #2

The earth will be renewed as we believe
And then become a shining paradise
A place where it and people can receive
A glory paid for with an awful price.

That glory, wholly sanctified and sure
All clean and free of sin and any stain
Transparent as a sea of glass and pure
Where future, past and present meld and reign.

And nothing that's impure abides the light
The slightest flaws are burned away by grace
White hot, to finish anything not right
To everything that is, a warm embrace.

Him crucified and bearing every sin
Invites us to repent and enter in.

D&C 78:19
19 And he who receiveth all things with thankfulness shall be made glorious; and the things of this earth shall be added unto him, even an hundred fold, yea, more.

Sonnet 809 D&C 78:19

We sing about the blessings we should count
Of listing our good fortunes one by one
Of how rewards in heaven will surmount
Afflictions and the insults to us done.

And gratitude remembered for the good
Is solace to the victims of real pain
But thinking that a list of blessings could
Remove real troubles is a hope in vain.

The way to overcome a load of care
Is rather to accept it as a gift
Receive in thankfulness all things you bear
Not just the things that give an easy lift.

When everything you get, you're thankful for
The ROI's * a hundred fold or more

*Return on Investment

Sonnet 810 D&C 78:19 #2

A certified financial planning guy
Is parked in every branch of every bank
Explaining which investments you should buy
He knows the rates and risks and how they rank.

But often things don't happen like they should
And markets will collapse and bonds will fail
And even when the guesswork turns out good
The pace of growth is usually like a snail.

But here's a better tip for high returns
For adding up the things of earth to you
A guarantee of glory while it earns
A hundred fold in blessings to accrue.

And all you have to do is show your thanks
You won't get this advice at any banks.

D&C 82:10
10 I, the Lord, am bound when ye do what I say; but when ye do not what I say, ye have no promise.

Sonnet 811 D&C 82:10

"I Did it My Way" What a song!
That anthem of defiant selfishness
Confusing soundly what is right from wrong
That narcissistic hymn of self excess.

"I Did it My Way" What a joke!
A nasty exclamation by a brat
An opportunity gone up in smoke
So fully out of tune, both sharp and flat.

"I Did it My Way" What a waste!
Mistaking bluster for courageousness
Exalting in a life so hubris based
It celebrates the wanting to transgress.

"I'll Do it His Way" That's the song!
A hymn to which we all should sing along.

Sonnet 812 D&C 82:10 #2

God keeps a promise. That's just how He is
His word is good. His bond a binding sure
The covenants that matter are all His
The promised blessings open and secure.

Do as I say, He says, and so it is
The burden of decision falls to you
The real rewards that matter are all His
His blessings ascertained by what you do.

The promise of a man is what he is
His character determined by his bond
The measure and the means supremely his
To settle where he fits in life beyond.

If you won't keep a promise here below
Then heaven's is not the place you're bound to go.

D&C 88:124
124 Cease to be idle; cease to be unclean; cease to find fault one with another; cease to sleep longer than is needful; retire to thy bed early, that ye may not be weary; arise early, that your bodies and your minds may be invigorated.

Sonnet 813 D&C 88:124 Cease to be Idle

To "cease", in general, means to desist
To put the brakes on something in a spin
To stop, to quit, to end. But here's the twist
To cease in idleness is to begin.

To overcome, by will, inertia's hold
Submitting to the Maker's call thereof
By actions calculated and so bold
They lift you up to works of faith and love.

Because the curse of idleness is not
The worst of all the ways to be untrue
Remember that unless our time is fraught
With good, that idleness might better do.

So go ahead and cease your idle ways
But don't replace your sloth with sinful days.

Sonnet 814 D&C 88:124 #2 Cease to be Unclean

The unclean of the world used to be
The lepers and diseased upon the street
Required to declare it by decree
"Unclean! Unclean!" they loudly must repeat.

And being thus compelled to so exclaim
Though ever in their hearts was the desire
To cease to be unclean and lose the shame
Of living in a physical hellfire.

But filthiness of heart prevails today
And unlike lepers, many hell bound folk
Have no desire to cease to be that way
And look upon repentance as a joke.

Those shamelessly promoting the obscene
Might just as well be shouting out "Unclean!"

Sonnet 815 D&C 88:124 #3 Cease to Find Fault

I wonder where the notion gets it's birth
That we can lift ourselves by tearing down
That somehow we increase inherent worth
By knocking off the other fellow's crown.

There is enough of actual fault within
My own imperfect life, filled to the brim
It keeps me busy weeding out my sin
My neighbour's faults I'll have to leave to him.

And ceasing to find fault with all my friends
Should give me time to see them as I should
Then both of us can better make amends
With focus not of fault, but on the good.

I doubt that by my ceasing to find fault
I'll somehow slow their progress to exalt.

Sonnet 816 D&C 88:124 #4 Cease to Sleep

It's not so much the sleep that's wrong to do
We have to have our rest, that's just the deal
But here is where the whole thing goes askew
It's when we go to sleep while at the wheel.

Some failures cannot ever be reversed
There will be time for sleep and other fun
But work and obligations must come first
And sleeping on the job won't get it done.

And choices must be made by me and you
Those times to step up and decide just which
Of all the things that matter we should do
Let's hope we're not found sleeping at the switch.

So get your sleep, but get it when you should
Not when you could be out there doing good.

D&C 89:18-21
18 And all saints who remember to keep and do these sayings, walking in obedience to the commandments, shall receive health in their navel and marrow to their bones;
19 And shall find wisdom and great treasures of knowledge, even hidden treasures;
20 And shall run and not be weary, and shall walk and not faint.
21 And I, the Lord, give unto them a promise, that the destroying angel shall pass by them, as the children of Israel, and not slay them. Amen.

Sonnet 817 D&C 89:18-21

The interview is simple and quite short
To give you entrance to the Lord's abode
The questions very measured with import
The highest earthly blessings there bestowed.

The wisdom and great treasures there abound
The weariness of life is there dismissed
And promises of every sort are found
The joy of the Spirit in our midst.

And none of this is given without this
The answer to a question that is true
A key to earthly tasting of a bliss
That without temples only heaven knew.

"The word of wisdom, do you keep it right?"
"Oh yes!" you cry. To enter this delight.

Sonnet 818 D&C 89:18-21 #2

The daily headlines do betray a trend
Of conflicts sadly clearly unresolved
Where when a friend is beaten by a friend
There must have been some alcohol involved.

And often accidents are quite bizarre
And so we say the tragedy evolved
Not by the fault of bus or truck or car
There must have been some alcohol involved.

Or sometimes younger people pass away
Their health and vigour seemingly dissolved
And looking at their cause of death we say
There must have been some alcohol involved.

Don't let this be how your fate gets resolved:
There must have been some alcohol involved.

Sonnet 819 D&C 89:18-21 #3

We talk about an athlete training hard
And speak of short term pain for long term gain
But keep the word of wisdom in regard
And gains are short and long and there's no pain.

The genius of this conduct is sublime
A blessing to a people quite immense
No headlines of insane or violent time
Less trouble and less ludicrous expense.

And all this wisdom settles social place
Away from vice below and vice above
A moderate and middle course of grace
Where humble souls can feel the Father's love.

How happy are the saints who learn to give
Obedience to wisdom's way to live!

D&C 107:8
8 The Melchizedek Priesthood holds the right of presidency, and has power and authority over all the offices in the church in all ages of the world, to administer in spiritual things.

Sonnet 820 D&C 107:8

We sing in praise of prophets and give thanks
For presidents who guide us in our days
We marvel to have priesthood in our ranks
To teach and bless and organize our ways.

The power and authority is great
The same that made the heavens and the earth
Preparing and extending as we wait
For that return of true eternal worth.

In matters of the Spirit we defer
To all the keys of priesthood held today
The same as what all ages did confer
Administering the Church in heaven's way.

And all the saints uphold with faithful care
The prophet by our confidence and prayer.

Sonnet 821 D&C 107:8 #2

The people of each stake are gathered twice
Each year to hear the words of life and do
Such business as by officers suffice
To all our faith and confidence renew.

And oft times there are speakers that we love
With messages so timely, wise and great
We learn and feel the powers from above
Renewed by better knowledge of our state.

Yet all this teaching only lasts a while
And needs each conf'rence time to be redone
New visitors, new music and new style
New programs, always once again begun.

But those new elders! There's a lasting note
Eternal priesthood power with one vote.

D&C 121:36,41-42

36 That the rights of the priesthood are inseparably connected with the powers of heaven, and that the powers of heaven cannot be controlled nor handled only upon the principles of righteousness.

41 No power or influence can or ought to be maintained by virtue of the priesthood, only by persuasion, by long-suffering, by gentleness and meekness, and by love unfeigned;

42 By kindness, and pure knowledge, which shall greatly enlarge the soul without hypocrisy, and without guile—

Sonnet 821 D&C 121:36,41-42

We see the awful power of brute force
The crushing strength of anger, pride and guile
The sharpness of deceit without remorse
Persuading by the preaching of revile.

Though none of this connects with heaven's power
On earth it has a fearful savage way
And tempts the weak and greedy hour by hour
To rule through aggression day by day.

The currencies of kindness and of love
Of patience and of meekness and increase
Of gentleness and yearnings for above
Are not enough alone to purchase peace.

But when combined with priesthood power's might
They'll vanquish earthly evil's awful blight.

Sonnet 822 D&C 121:36,41-42 #2

The reverence God has for agency
Is by this simple scripture verse explained
"No power... can," by priesthood's virtue be
Controlled, influenced, handled or maintained.

The pow'r that made the heavens and the earth
That set the stars and planets in their place
That guides the very miracle of birth
Is only exercised through love and grace.

Yet natural man must learn this virtue here
Perhaps the best of God's enduring love
To set aside the tools of force and fear
In favour of persuasion from above.

Be careful as you practice priesthood arts
To use these gentle ways to turn men's hearts.

D&C 130:22-23
22 The Father has a body of flesh and bones as tangible as man's; the Son also; but the Holy Ghost has not a body of flesh and bones, but is a personage of Spirit. Were it not so, the Holy Ghost could not dwell in us.
23 A man may receive the Holy Ghost, and it may descend upon him and not tarry with him.

Sonnet 823 D&C 130:22-23 The Holy Ghost

A Messenger, a Friend, a Witness too
A Testifier, Spirit, and a Guide
The Verifier of the good and true
A Comfort touching deep and warm inside.

A Light, a Teacher, and a Still Small Voice
Instructing, calling, warning and supplied
The Holy Spirit, Arbiter of choice
A Comfort touching deep and warm inside.

Companion and a Sanctifier true
The Agent of repentance when applied
The Holy Ghost affirms what you should do
A Comfort touching deep and warm inside.

The Burning in the Bosom's never lied
A Comfort touching deep and warm inside.

Sonnet 824 D&C 130:22-23 #2 The Son

The Author and Creator of All Things
The Finisher of Faith and Faithful Friend
Beloved Son of God and King of Kings
The Cornerstone, Beginning and the End.

The Bright and Morning Star, Anointed One
Jehovah and the Seed of Abraham
Begotten, Endless and Beloved Son
The Shepherd and the Healer, Son of Man.

The Way, the Light, the Life, the Prince, the Stone
The Savior of the World, Eternal Head
The Son, the Rock, the Word in Flesh and Bone
Eternal Judge of All the Quick and Dead.

The Everlasting Father and the Lamb
The Christ, the Mighty God, the Great I Am.

Sonnet 825 D&C 130: 22-23 #3 The Father

Oh Father. God of Heaven and the earth
Oh Father. Blessed Source of life and all
Oh Father. Hope of everyone's rebirth
Oh Father. Send me Comfort when I fall.

Oh Father. Master of the universe
Oh Father. Maker of the great and small
Oh Father. Healer, Counsellor, and nurse
Oh Father. Hear my asking when I call.

Oh Father. With thy kind all seeing eye
Oh Father. Guide me home when I am lost
Oh Father. Please accept my feeble try
Oh Father. Help me understand the cost.

Oh Father. Send forgiveness when I sin.
Oh Father. Cleanse my vessel from within.

D&C 131:1-4

1 In the celestial glory there are three heavens or degrees;

2 And in order to obtain the highest, a man must enter into this order of the priesthood [meaning the new and everlasting covenant of marriage];

3 And if he does not, he cannot obtain it.

4 He may enter into the other, but that is the end of his kingdom; he cannot have an increase.

Sonnet 826 D&C 131:1-4

All these are valiant followers of Christ
The anxiously engaged with might and mind
Resisting gladly when by sin enticed
Their hearts and strength by love of God entwined.

And these are happy, bless-ed, kind and good
Engrained with gratitude for everything
Desiring only to do what they should
Full throated in their praise of God they sing.

Obedience the measure of their ways
And any sacrifice without complaint
Their faith the constant watchword of their days
They pray to God believing without feint.

Celestial glory, heaven's highest place
It doesn't cost, it pays, to earn that grace.

Sonnet 827 D&C 131:1-4

And here again the irony is strong
Rewarding up in heaven by this plan
To do the thing that best makes life a song
And come together as a wife and man.

You might expect some test that's arduous
To earn you "top of class" in heaven's place
But no, the thing that works is marvellous
A marriage made in covenants of grace.

And is it not this way with all commands?
We're told to do just what we should desire
The wise man learns and fully understands
That righteousness will always lift us higher.

Amazing that we prove ourselves in this
By taking on the joys of wedded bliss.

JS-H 1:15-20

15 After I had retired to the place where I had previously designed to go, having looked around me, and finding myself alone, I kneeled down and began to offer up the desires of my heart to God. I had scarcely done so, when immediately I was seized upon by some power which entirely overcame me, and had such an astonishing influence over me as to bind my tongue so that I could not speak. Thick darkness gathered around me, and it seemed to me for a time as if I were doomed to sudden destruction.

16 But, exerting all my powers to call upon God to deliver me out of the power of this enemy which had seized upon me, and at the very moment when I was ready to sink into despair and abandon myself to destruction—not to an imaginary ruin, but to the power of some actual being from the unseen world, who had such marvellous power as I had never before felt in any being—just at this moment of great alarm, I saw a pillar of light exactly over my head, above the brightness of the sun, which descended gradually until it fell upon me.

17 It no sooner appeared than I found myself delivered from the enemy which held me bound. When the light rested upon me I saw two Personages, whose brightness and glory defy all description, standing above me in the air. One of them spake unto me, calling me by name and said, pointing to the other—This is My Beloved Son. Hear Him!

18 My object in going to inquire of the Lord was to know which of all the sects was right, that I might know which to join. No sooner, therefore, did I get possession of myself, so as to be able to speak, than I

asked the Personages who stood above me in the light, which of all the sects was right (for at this time it had never entered into my heart that all were wrong)—and which I should join.

19 I was answered that I must join none of them, for they were all wrong; and the Personage who addressed me said that all their creeds were an abomination in his sight; that those professors were all corrupt; that: "they draw near to me with their lips, but their hearts are far from me, they teach for doctrines the commandments of men, having a form of godliness, but they deny the power thereof."

20 He again forbade me to join with any of them; and many other things did he say unto me, which I cannot write at this time. When I came to myself again, I found myself lying on my back, looking up into heaven. When the light had departed, I had no strength; but soon recovering in some degree, I went home. And as I leaned up to the fireplace, mother inquired what the matter was. I replied, "Never mind, all is well—I am well enough off." I then said to my mother, "I have learned for myself that Presbyterianism is not true." It seems as though the adversary was aware, at a very early period of my life, that I was destined to prove a disturber and an annoyer of his kingdom; else why should the powers of darkness combine against me? Why the opposition and persecution that arose against me, almost in my infancy?

Sonnet 828 JS-H 1:15-20

Exposed to any story such as this
A listener may wonder if it's true
If this is something safely to dismiss
Or should it be a thing to look into?

All sorts of folks have heard this tale by now
Have listened and considered and resolved
And many, in the millions, do avow
The truth of all assertions here involved.

And this should give you pause enough to test
If learning for yourself is easy done
And if you could be thusly also blessed
With knowledge of the Father and the Son.

Go find a sacred closet of your own
It's there the truth of heaven will be shown.

Sonnet 828 JS-H 1:15-20 #2

Of course the devil made his fruitless ploy
His shadow giving to the coming light
A backdrop meant, the vision, to destroy
Yet only made the outcome shine more bright.

An unseen actual being fully felt
An enemy, a force, a frantic move
Against a child who dared in faith, and knelt
Unknowing of what wonder this would prove.

And then! A pillared light. The darkness done
Two persons in the air. He hears his name
Then Father introducing Christ the Son
And nothing, nothing, nothing is the same.

This boy, delivered now from dark despair
Was ready for the answer to his prayer.

Sonnet 829 JS-H 1:15-20 #3

Young Joseph found his sacred grove nearby
No pilgrimage or quest or search was done
No gilded trappings but the morning sky
No other witness than the springtime sun.

And simple faith, and simple study too
That's all that was required to prepare
A simple boy for what the Lord would do
In answer to his simple humble prayer.

And this is but a pattern for us each
A shape of how to gain the Father's voice
The proof of heaven's willingness to teach
The outcome governed by the simplest choice.

So if you have some faith and real desire
Just pick some quiet place and then enquire.

Sonnet 830 JS-H 1:15-20 #4

The parsing and the picking of the nits
In any sort of testament of fact
Becomes a battle of contestants' wits
Until the truth is lost in the abstract.

You cannot hope to know it by these means
The fabric of the past is far too torn
And shadows cast upon competing scenes
Obscure our vision of the story sworn.

So how you gonna know if this is true
If Joseph's testimony can't prevail
If argument and evidence won't do
What will expose the truth of such a tale.

When you receive these things you have to pray
And get the same instruction, the same way.

Sonnet 831 JS-H 1:15-20 #5

Oh mysteries of earth and fire and rock
You nevermore will be to us the same
The very dust now quickened to unlock
The truth which sets an honest heart aflame.

The trees that saw the boy step humbly in
And stood in wonder as they must have felt
At least a part of what would now begin
When just a boy in prayer so faithful knelt.

In shadows were his boyish features caught
His mission one to overcome a doubt
Then light in pillar blazoned overwrought
A boy steps in. A prophet's coming out!

So Joseph's face returned to morning light
Out of the grove. And now! The end of night!

Bonus Scripture D&C 130:20-21

**20 There is a law, irrevocably decreed in heaven before the foundations of this world, upon which all blessings are predicated—
 21 And when we obtain any blessing from God, it is by obedience to that law upon which it is predicated.**

Sonnet 832 D&C 130:20-21

The blessings cannot ever be in doubt
Their promise is decreed by heaven's law
It's not so hard to find the process out
The outcomes are delivered without flaw.

The mystery is why we go so wrong
With clear instructions kindly all around
And guidance for the sinner all along
No blessing should be forfeit or unfound.

And do we have examples of the fate
Of those who flaunt the laws of consequence?
Of course we do, and yet we still debate
Devoid, it seems of simple common sense.

Obey the law! That's what you have to do
And heaven's consequence will come to you.

Made in the USA
San Bernardino, CA
19 April 2014